MW00628723

SOMETHING TO CHEER ABOUT

SOMETHING TO CHEER ABOUT

Legends from the Golden Age of Sports

Jack McDonald

With a Foreword by Mel Durslag

A Harvest/HBJ Book

HARCOURT BRACE JOVANOVICH, PUBLISHERS

San Diego   New York   London

Copyright © 1986 by Jack McDonald
Foreword copyright © 1986 by Mel Durslag

Requests for permission to make copies of any part of the work
should be mailed to: Permissions, Harcourt Brace Jovanovich,
Publishers, Orlando, Florida 32887.

Library of Congress Cataloging-in-Publication Data
McDonald, Jack.
Something to cheer about.
"A Harvest/HBJ book."
1. Sports—United States—History.   I. Title.
GV583.M34   1986   796'.0973   86-9995
ISBN 0-15-683804-4

Designed by Francesca M. Smith
Printed in the United States of America
First Harvest/HBJ edition 1986
A B C D E F G H I J

Contents

Foreword

IT IS A TRIBUTE to the world of letters that Jack McDonald predates the word processor. Jack makes money the old-fashioned way—he earns it on a typewriter.

The typewriter Jack uses is a beautiful instrument. It requires no electrical outlets. Its keyboard may be discussed in earthly terms, not in terms of Ks and memory capacities. With the errant press of a single button a typewriter's whole compositions cannot be expunged.

One day the typewriter will come back and the world will camp on Jack's doorstep, pleading for instruction in the use of the marvelous invention he has employed for more than sixty years now in creating his familiar, fascinating prose.

The age of Jack will not be revealed here, mainly because it is easier to pry from Coca-Cola the secret of its formula than to dredge from Jack his vintage. Suffice it to say that in the service of his government he sailed on the U.S.S. *Mt. Vernon* in 1918. By 1926 he could be found in San Francisco, tilling an oar in the sports department of the old *Call Bulletin*.

The time once existed in American journalism when newspapers could be counted on to outlast their writers. Regrettably, that condition in many instances has been reversed, explaining Jack's appearance in what would become the *News-Call Bulletin*, and, later, in the *San Francisco Examiner*.

During his roaring incumbency, there was little in sports that he missed. It was the World Series, the Kentucky Derby, the

U.S. Open, the Rose Bowl, the Olympic Games, the championship boxing matches of his time. He bounced from Dempsey to Ruth to Stengel to DiMaggio.

The cigar he smoked filled the nostrils of Eddie Arcaro, Willie Shoemaker, Helen Wills, Sugar Ray Robinson, and Arnold Palmer. And young authors wondering idly about Sonja Henie knew precisely whom to contact.

Jack saw it all, moving about in a rollicking period of sports journalism, carbonated by competition, distantly removed from the quiet scene prevailing today.

The toll on the prolific press of McDonald's heyday continues unabated . . . three major dailies in New York, two in Boston . . . two in Chicago . . . two in Philadelphia . . . two in Los Angeles . . . two in San Francisco . . . one in Washington, D.C. . . . countless monopolies elsewhere. In such an atmosphere, the Jack McDonalds yawn.

On January 25, 1968, they tossed a retirement party for Jack in San Francisco. They sprang for prime rib of eastern beef, Coupe San Francisco, petit fours, sec, and appropriate wines. And some of sports' most distinguished characters rose to bid bon voyage to the rascal, whom they figured to be heading for pasture on the way to entering into rest.

What Jack forgot to tell them was that he was taking their dinner under fraudulent pretense. No sooner did he down the eastern prime rib than he set up shop as a travel writer. From a base near Guadalajara, Mexico, he launched a new career, calling on ports of the world and dispatching accounts to a collection of choice clients he put together. Then he went on to author a book on his war experiences, entitled *Navy Retread*. And now he puts together his sports memories, based on more than four decades of adventure on the planet Jock.

It has long been the feeling here that athletes, coaches, and managers announcing their retirement should post a bond, to be forfeited when they return. The money would be used for selected refreshments for all those attending the retirement press conference and for wiping moisture from their eyes in print over the departure of old and revered heroes.

Under this plan, applied to the literati, Jack McDonald would be subject to forfeiture. When he bade adios in 1968, evoking warm nostalgia, if not a tear, from his pals, he offered no hint of the vast outpouring of written language that would follow.

In a recent note to me, Jack lamented that most of his buddies were now gone. Among those remaining, he said, I was doing best of all. I had suffered only a heart attack.

—Mel Durslag

Introduction

SOMETHING TO CHEER ABOUT. Why the title? Down the sports trail Jack McDonald traveled for forty-two years as a sportswriter, editor, and columnist in San Francisco. One of a mere handful who covers a span from the Mauve Decade of the Roaring Twenties to the present day, he had intimate friendships with Ruth, Gehrig, Dempsey, Cobb, Bobby Jones, Helen Wills, Red Grange, and other giants of the Golden Age of Sports.

Jack harks back to the days when all sports, pro and amateur, were fun and entertainment. Were those athletes of yesteryear really different from those of today? The answer is their images surely were, and for good reason.

This was before once-friendly smiles had been wiped off of athletes' faces by multimillion-dollar contracts, lawyers and lawsuits, player strikes, artificial turf and domed stadiums, franchise shifts, and billion-dollar TV deals. Even more important, drugs had yet to make their unseemly intrusion onto the playing fields.

In those golden years and until relatively recently, writers felt an obligation, when writing of the shining knights of the playing field, to create an illusion about them. It was an unwritten law (but one rigidly adhered to) that this illusion should be created and preserved. Some would call it a cover-up not to delve into the private lives, nocturnal activities, and other frailties of sports heroes. These men weren't angels—many had feet of clay.

But illusion was deemed essential, something to be fostered and respected. And with very little radio and no television, image was in the hands of the sportswriter.

Besides, there were more wholesome things to write about the athletes of yesterday. More country bumpkins—"you-know-me-Al" characters—were around. They weren't well paid and the idea of too much money getting them into trouble was not a factor. In fact, the style of the sportswriter of bygone days was to feature human and wholesome rollicking color rather than personal dirt, which was left to the scandal tabloids.

The writers drew from a limitless well of personal experiences with the sports giants of their day: the Ruths, Dempseys, et al. In its purest essence, nostalgia is not a salable item, but McDonald, with his imaginative yet introspective bent, traveled the trains with Casey Stengel, was in a hotel room with barnstorming Ruth and Gehrig when they chased each other around in shorts flicking backsides with wet towels, and had to double as Jack Dempsey on a sports program in the pioneer days of radio.

A pro in every sense of the word, McDonald, in addition to his style and wit, never forgot for a moment that the most important skill of a sportswriter is primarily to be a good reporter. He asked questions and took ample notes, and was always where the action was. This shows in his book. He covered more than a score of World Series, Kentucky Derbies, and world heavyweight championships—"ring battles" as well as the passing parade of routine, "rainy-day," off-season periods of sports, writing when nothing in particular was happening and one had to avoid boring the reader.

It was a clue to his ability that before he took over the baseball beat on the old San Francisco *Call Bulletin* in mid-season, he'd never in his life covered a game. Yet he became one of its most prolific and knowledgeable reporters. In horse racing, too, he was a complete neophyte at the start but became a nationally recognized turf authority.

McDonald's writing belongs to America. He has dug deep into his memories and pulled many delicious anecdotes, never before published, about bygone years and storybook stars to put into this book. Characters he writes about are truly "something to cheer about." To this day he retains the knack of making the great athletes of yesteryear and their most memorable moments come vividly to life. Reading this book is a must for both advanced sports followers and the average fan.

(It was the creed of the old-time sportswriter to entertain above all, while also being factual. Piece on it as you please, start at the beginning, middle, or near the end.) He has made every page entertaining with his amazing memory and tale-telling style.

SOMETHING TO CHEER ABOUT

Writers of the
Roaring Twenties

I COUNT MYSELF fortunate to have come along the sportswriting pike midway in the Roaring Twenties, the so-called Golden Age of Sports, which Westbrook Pegler translated into the "Era of Wonderful Nonsense." It spawned some great sportswriters during the lives and times of Jack Dempsey, Babe Ruth, Ty Cobb, Bobby Jones, Red Grange, Earl Sande, and, on the women's side, Helen Wills and Suzanne Lenglen. Sports copy could hardly be dull with these skillful people to write about.

Good sportswriters are creative. This era had them in abundance, but it's not easy to choose the best. There are no batting averages, knockout records, pass completion percentages, or earned averages by which to assay knights of the typewriter. Perhaps Damon Runyon is the best remembered. He was contemporaneous with Grantland Rice, Paul Gallico, Ring Lardner, Bugs Baer, Bill Corum, John Kieran, Pegler, and others. Each had his own style.

Runyon wrote showcase stuff. He was at home covering a war, big murder trial, Sing Sing execution, heavyweight title fight, World Series, or Kentucky Derby. Although basically a sportswriter, he turned to sports after a hitch on the city side. As a teenage GI, he served in the Philippines, and after the Aguinaldo Rebellion there worked on the old *San Francisco Post*.

His coverage of the Bruno Hauptman trial for kidnapping the Lindbergh baby and such others as the Hall-Mills and Judd-Gray murder cases was outstanding, but his big contributions

1

to literature were his fiction stories about Broadway's guys and dolls. His characters were frequenters of the bookie joints and boxing gyms. They were fictitious, but he painted them with authentic jargon.

For years, *Colliers*, a top national magazine, took anything he wrote on sight, paying him five thousand dollars per story, no matter how short. Boxing, baseball, and horse racing were his favorite sports. His "Never a Handy Guy like Sande" Derby story was a particular masterpiece.

Runyon never got beyond the fourth grade. He acquired his education hanging around newspaper offices where his dad was a tramp printer. His handling of sports jargon was so unique *Webster's* had to coin a new word: *Runyonese*.

I met Runyon in San Francisco during the Treasure Island World's Fair. He was stopping at the old Palace Hotel just across from the *Call Bulletin*, on New Montgomery Street and Jessie. He had just come back from Caesar Martinelli's in North Beach, where he'd had a spaghetti dinner with garlic butter and parsley sauce, the likes of which he'd never tasted before. He was in his room batting out a short story about a character named Horse Thief Burke who kept taking aspirin tablets—not for a headache, but "just in case I should get one." Runyon could take a smidgen of an idea and puff it up into a corking short story in his inimitable style. Many tried to imitate it, always without success.

As a stylist Ring Lardner was right up there with Runyon. Maybe Ring came closer to being a genius than any of his contemporaries. His humor was tremendous, and his piece about the last game pitched by tuberculosis-wracked Christy Mathewson, which I read as a boy, brought tears. "The Champion" was an all-time great sports fiction yarn, and the "you-know-me-Al" stories about a semiliterate bush leaguer set a pattern by which players were stamped for a generation. As a "dialogue man" Ring had no peer in sportswriting.

Over several decades nobody made a greater success of sportswriting than Grantland Rice. A graduate of Vanderbilt, he brought a "southern gentleman" theme into sports. Granny knew the sports figures he wrote about intimately. Fair play was his creed, but he wasn't stuffy. Nobody liked a laugh or party better. A student of Greek and Latin as well as football and baseball, he was also an outstanding versifier, often starting a story with a short poem.

It was Rice who named the Four Horsemen of Notre Dame in perhaps his best-remembered story of the same title. It went: "Outlined against the blue-gray October sky the Four Horsemen rode again. In dramatic lore they were known as Famine, Pestilence, Destruction, and Death. These are but aliases. Their real names are Stuhldreher, Miller, Crowley, and Layden. They are the crest of the South Bend cyclone (the Notre Dame backfield) before which another fighting West Point army football team was swept over the precipice of the Polo Grounds here today."

Rice dealt in a lot of allegorical stuff and symbols and was a great one for choosing mythical subjects and applying them to sports figures for dramatization. And he was good at it. In his prime he was the most widely read and respected sports chronicler in the country, and he developed a following without once having blasted an athlete in print.

But my Mr. Wonderful among all the headliners was Bill Corum—my idol. Corum had a style all his own. I drank in every word he ever wrote. If any of it rubbed off on me I was a better writer for it. One night during a World Series, Bill said, "I don't want to be a millionaire; I just want to live like one." None of us listeners were within $999,000 of being a millionaire, but we all felt we were living like ones, writing sports. The fact that Bill, the youngest major in World War I, and I had been in France together added to our bond of friendship.

3

He died in 1958 before completing his book of memoirs. He didn't lack for material—his sports thrills had included Whirlaway's great Derby win, the epic Dempsey-Firpo fight, and Grover Cleveland Alexander's great win over the Yankees. The night before he died, he whispered, "Keep me going just a few more days, doc, till I finish my book. That's all I ask." Bill didn't quite make it, but buddies put on the finishing touches.

Paul Gallico was a great sportswriter. His *Farewell to Sports* stood up for years as one of the better sports books. He wasn't immensely popular with average sports-page readers because he wrote over their heads. He either couldn't or wouldn't write down to them.

Pegler wrote with great humor when he started out in sports, but when he branched out into political fields he developed a bilious approach. When he greeted Suzanne Lenglen, the French tennis queen, at the dock one morning, others wrote of her playing style. Not Pegler—he went back and batted out a piece, not in the best of taste, about what a great matrimonial venture it would be from a eugenics standpoint if Suzanne and Red Grange got hitched and raised a family.

Henry McLemore was one of the most humorous sportswriters of his time. He was a chronic picker of losers, and was so sure Max Baer would clobber Jim Braddock in 1935 he wrote that if Baer lost, he would go to India and live in exile. The next day his story had a Rangoon dateline and told of his house hunting.

Bugs Baer was the funniest sports scribe in print. He was inimitable and could conjure up more similes—uproarious ones—in a single column than most other writers could create in a year. Other good writers in New York were Bill McGeehan (a former San Franciscan), the versatile Bob Considine, Heywood Broun, Joe Williams, Arthur Daley, Jimmy Cannon, Tom Meany, Davis Walsh, Hype Igoe, and Quentin Reynolds.

The Babe Was a Pip

I BROKE IN AS a baseball writer on the old San Francisco *Call* in the era of Babe Ruth. My first story was about Ping Bodie, whose real name was Francesco Stefano Pezzolo. I believe he was the first Italian to play in the majors, the forerunner of the Lazzeris, Berras, Cimolis, and Crosettis—not to mention the DiMaggios.

He changed his name to Ping Bodie because his dad had been a gold miner in the old mother lode town of Bodie. This first baseball yarn was based on a question I asked Ping about what it was like to be a roommate of Babe Ruth.

"I roomed with a suitcase," he laughed. "About the only time I saw him was at the ballpark or on a train. He couldn't come through a hotel lobby without being mobbed by fans. If he ate at the hotel, diners pestered him for autographs and his food got cold. I got to know him best on sleeper jumps. He loved to play poker. First thing he'd do on boarding the train would be to peel off his jacket and shirt and holler for a deck of cards.

"As the evening wore on he'd want something to eat. One night the porter dug up a mass of spareribs and sauerkraut and a case of beer. At the next stop a crowd gathered and demanded that the Babe come out on the rear platform, which he did—in his shorts and bedroom slippers, spareribs in one hand, bottle of beer in the other. The crowd loved it.

"I followed Ruth in the batting order. I used to hate to see him hit a homer because when I did, the pitcher would take it

5

out on me. I'd yell, 'Hey, why take it out on me? I didn't hit it.'

"But they'd hiss, 'Get up you busher so I can knock you down again!' "

A year after this interview Ruth hit his sixty homers and came to San Francisco, where I met him for the first time. The 1927 season had just ended, and our meeting took place under unique circumstances. He was mischievous and friendly as a puppy.

Ruth was in town with his teammate Lou Gehrig. The two were en route to Japan for an exhibition tour. Before sailing, they had signed to play several exhibition games at old Recreation Park.

Arriving at the door of their hotel room, "Putty" (George Putnam, part owner of the San Francisco Seals) and I heard a loud commotion inside—chairs crashing to the floor, a dressing table sliding across the room, divans being overturned, and yells of laughter and pain from within. Putty rapped real hard several times. Finally, we heard the gruff (though good-natured) voice of Ruth inside as he shouted, "C'mon in!"

As we entered I noticed the place was a shambles. Ruth was still chasing Gehrig around the room. The Babe had showered. Clad only in shorts, they were snapping big, wet Turkish towels at each other's backsides. This went on until they were exhausted. Then Ruth looked at us and grinned. Dropping his towel, he toddled across the room on those spindly legs of his and, with mincing steps, came over and shook hands with Putnam. Then he gave me a good-natured "Hiya, kid" as Putty introduced me.

It was raining buckets outside and this was costing Babe and Lou money, for they were getting a big percentage of the gate, but Babe was happy at not having to suit up. "I hope it rains for a month," he laughed. "It has been a long, tiring season."

Patiently, he answered my somewhat immature, amateurish

questions, such as how many home runs he expected to hit next season. He predicted he would retire in five more years. While this was doubtless just a guess for him at the time, it was exactly what happened. While we talked, he was dressing.

Finally, when he was all slicked up, patent leather shoes (the rage at the time) and all, he growled at Gehrig as only he could, "Hey, you, gimme some do-re-mi; I'm going out on the town tonight."

The two had a joint bankroll. Neither kept track of how much was in it or who spent what, where, and when. Gehrig reached into his open grip and fished out a roll of bills big enough for an elephant to choke on. They were kept intact by a big, wide rubber band. The roll had to be at least six inches in circumference and it was packed tight with fives, tens, and some fifties, too.

Lou grabbed the roll, cocked an arm, and flung it at Babe, who ducked. It hit the edge of the open window nine stories above the rainswept street. An inch higher and it would have gone sailing down. "You dirty SOB," roared Babe, playfully. He picked up the currency and removed the rubber band, snatched a fistful of bills (not even bothering to count them), and stuck them carelessly into his pants pockets. He could have taken a thousand dollars out of the wad; neither seemed to care a hoot. They kept no books. He put the rubber band back on and fired the roll back at Gehrig, who also ducked. This time it hit the bathroom wall and fell into the tub, where Gehrig picked it up dripping wet, and was heaved carelessly back into the open grip.

The next afternoon, the two suited up and Ruth hit about twenty straight batting-practice pitches over the fence for a starter. Skeptics claimed he brought along his own superlively, trick baseballs that would sail farther than the regulation kind.

He parked three balls over the church roof just outside right field and into the street, where kids waited to retrieve them.

The balls, I learned, were standard Coast League spheroids. Some claimed the Seals pitchers had frozen them to deaden their life.

After hitting four homers during the game, Ruth showered down and then came into a little private dining room where Dr. Charles H. Strub, Charlie Graham, and Putnam waited with us writers, Messrs. Kemp, Laird, Hughes, and myself.

Putty, gourmand that he was, had prepared an elaborate spread of so-called hors d'oeuvres. By actual count, Ruth ate seven hot dogs, almost a whole platter of pig's feet, about ten slices of thick cold cuts, then excused himself with, "The grub was swell, gents." Grabbing the last pig's foot, he went on, "I hate to leave such a nice party so soon, honest, but I'm already late for a dinner engagement."

This was the Babe as I found him in his heyday. Nearly twenty years later when I saw him in San Francisco, he was wasting away with cancer, shortly before his death in 1945. I thought back to that afternoon at the Whitcomb when he stood there grinning and saying, "Hiya, kid."

The Ty Cobb I Knew

TY COBB, "the Georgia Peach," was the greatest all-around ball player of all time. He was the first man to be enshrined in the Hall of Fame at Cooperstown, having received more votes than the legendary Babe Ruth, Christy Mathewson, or Hans Wagner. When Ty hung up his spikes he had set eighty records. Some of them still stand and perhaps always will. For twelve seasons, nine of them in a row, he was the American League batting champion. He had a lifetime batting average of .367. One year alone he stole ninety-six bases. But he was more than a statistic or a set of them. On the field and off, he was a dynamic, sometimes ruthless, flaming-tempered, restless soul.

He lived most of the last thirty years of his life down on the San Francisco Peninsula, in Atherton. I was, you might say, his Boswell for most of those years until he went back to Georgia to die, and beneath a gruff, sometimes surly exterior beat a heart that was warm and human.

Early one morning in February, 1957, the phone rang in my home. The voice was Ty's. "He made it! He made it!" he blurted.

"Who made what?" I asked, only half awake.

"Why Crawford, old Wahoo Sam, the sonofagun. They just put him in the Hall of Fame!"

Nobody, including Sam himself, could have been more elated

than Ty. I know. I was privy to piles of correspondence at Ty's home, handwritten letters of appeal Ty had sent to influential baseball people on Crawford's behalf. Why? He and Sam had been bitter enemies on the Detroit Tigers. They hadn't spoken to each other in years.

"I'm going to write a story on how you have been working tirelessly for years to get Crawford into Cooperstown," I said.

"If you do, I'll never tell you another thing in confidence as long as I live," was the answer.

"All right, Ty, you win," I said. "I'll wait until the day you die to write it."

He agreed to that and that's the way it was. He had talked enthusiastically for years of the progress he was making toward getting Wahoo Sam in, always pledging me to secrecy. I often asked, "Why are you working so hard for a guy you hated and didn't speak to for years?"

"Because he merits the honor," was the reply. "Look at the man's record. He made the majors his first year in organized ball. Today with the lively ball, he'd be one of the greatest home-run hitters of all time. And he didn't go just for homers. He had a .300 lifetime average. He was a big burly guy, surely no antelope, yet he stole forty-one bases one season."

Ty would never discuss his feud with Crawford, even off the record, but Oscar Vitt, a teammate of both, told me it all stemmed from Sam's jealousy. "He would make three or four hits in a game and Cobb would steal home with the winning run to get all the headlines. For years they didn't speak. Sam always hit third and Ty fourth, in cleanup."

In the late 1930s a testimonial dinner was given for Ty at the old San Francisco Press Club. Among the honored guests were Grantland Rice, Gene Fowler, Henry McLemore, Pat O'Brien, and Guy Kibbee. That night Rice told a story about Ty. Long before the Georgia Peach got up to the big leagues,

10

Rice had written reams about him in the *Atlanta Journal*—even before he had seen him play. All the information on Cobb's amazing talents had been supplied by Ty himself, though Rice wasn't to learn this until years later. Ty was an eighteen-year-old rookie, then with the Anniston (Alabama) club. He bombarded Rice with telegrams. On the road, every time the train stopped Cobb would run into the station and send a telegram to Granny and sign it "Smith," "Jackson," or "Jones." "Watch this boy Cobb; he's a real comer" was the gist of them all.

Besieged with these messages, all from different towns and with different signatures, Rice had to be impressed. Then he started getting letters from Anniston, written in disguised, backhand penmanship but all authored by Ty. The missives supplied more details on this great phenom named Cobb. One read, "There's a young fellow on the Anniston club named Cobb who can do everything—field, run, hit, bunt, steal bases like a thief in the night. If you're smart you'll hop aboard his bandwagon because he's the greatest ball player ever to come out of the South and he is destined to become the diamond star of the ages, and he'll make a prophet of you."

Rice took to running these letters, adding flourishes of his own comment without yet having seen Ty play. His write-ups attracted big-league scouts and hastened Cobb's debut in the majors.

All of these fictitious letters make Ty look like a showboat. "I wrote them only for one reason," Ty told me later, and I believe him. He wanted to make sure his dad saw the glowing write-ups. His father was a strict, austere Scotch-Irish schoolteacher, also mayor of the town, and he had been dead set against his son going into baseball. "My dad wanted me to become a doctor," Ty said. "When I went into baseball he said to go ahead and get it out of my system and then come home and go to college.

"I wrote those letters about myself to Rice to bolster my own confidence and also show the old man I was making good. When I did make good he caved in and we became good pals. He gave me a lot of advice and most of it came from the Good Book."

Ty Cobb:
A Difficult Personality

I WONDER WHAT Tyrus Raymond Cobb would have to say about all the attention given the 4,192d base hit by Pete Rose. Of course, that's the one that broke the Georgia Peach's lifetime record of 4,191 hits.

Cobb left the game with about eighty individual records to his credit, many of which still stand, and he viewed his lifetime hits record as one of his proudest achievements. He showed this the day Stan Musial passed the 3,000 milestone and Cobb dictated a wire that began, "Welcome to the 3,000 Hit Club." It was, and still is, an exclusive society, and Cobb placed a high value on his 4,191.

I was a friend of Ty's for many years. He was a man of many minuses, and his difficult personality was such that if I was ever sentenced to spend the rest of my life on an uninhabited island with just one man for a companion, Cobb would never be the choice.

But he was also a man of many pluses, some of which he hid as if he wanted to be known as a bad guy. One big plus was his support of the battle for old-timers' pensions. To his dying day in 1961, he never did forgive the modern group of players for not including stars of the game prior to 1946 in the pension plan.

Of course, Cobb didn't need a pension. When he died, he left nine million dollars, including 95 percent of his fortune, to the hospital he founded. But right down to his dying breath he fought to get pensions for those he called "the forgotten men of baseball"—old-timers who had helped build the game into the big bonanza it has come to be.

Cobb deemed it a grave injustice that those who hung up their spikes prior to 1946 were left out in the cold. No provision whatsoever was made for them. It was inexcusable, he maintained, that young players, in their greedy eagerness to get security for themselves, gave no thought to the generation before them.

"It's high time," he declared, "they gave thought to older stars who played in the days of low salaries. Many of them saved their money but were wiped out in the 1929 stock market crash. These men were a powerful force in giving today's players the financial security they now enjoy.

"High-salaried players today can retire at an early age on fat pensions—money many of them will never need," Cobb once said. "Some of the money should have gone to the men who contributed so much to a game they got so little from in return."

Cobb also swung a heavy bat against the painfully slow system by which players who left the game prior to 1940 are denied admission to the Cooperstown Hall of Fame. "The gate is all but shut to many who should have been voted in long ago," Cobb contended.

Before they finally made it, Cobb fought tooth and nail to get Joe Sewell, Eppa Rixey, Sam Rice, Edd Roush, and his old Tigers teammate, Wahoo Sam Crawford, admitted.

"Why?" Cobb argued. "There are fellows in their late seventies waiting to be admitted. They built the game for the younger men who were chosen later. As a brother player, contemporaneous with their era, I know how they feel. This is not a modern players Hall of Fame. It belongs to those of a past generation also."

Cobb and Babe Ruth were the first to be admitted into

14

Cooperstown. Cobb cited Rixey as one of the forgotten men. "He won more games than any left-handed pitcher in the National League, up to the time he retired," Cobb said. "Here was a bona fide star who never pitched in the minors. He walked right off the University of Virginia grounds into a big-league uniform and finished with a brilliant twenty-one-year major league career."

Cobb showed me a handwritten letter he had received from Rixey (later voted in by an old timers' committee). It read; "Dear Ty, I am deeply grateful for your tireless effort in my behalf. That is a greater honor and compliment to me than being elected to the Hall of Fame, believe me."

One spring training in Arizona when Joe Sewell was in a Cleveland Indians coaching uniform, Ty nudged me, saying, "See that white-haired geezer over there? That's Joe Sewell. He's past seventy now and he's still on the waiting list for Cooperstown."

All Sewell did was strike out the fewest times of any player in his era—only 114 times in fifteen full seasons. That's about 8 times a year. Two of those seasons he fanned only 4 times. He was a shortstop, mind you, and wasn't supposed to be a great hitter, but he batted cleanup five seasons for Cleveland and his lifetime average was .312.

Cobb mentioned that after Sewell left Cleveland for the Yankees he hit in the number two spot just ahead of Ruth and Gehrig. He was third in all of baseball in consecutive games played, logging 1,110 straight.

After Ty's death, a national magazine called him a "pinch-penny." I wouldn't call him that, but neither could I rightly call him the last of the big spenders. The late Oscar Vitt and I once had dinner with Cobb in Sonoma, and I saw him tip the waiter ten dollars when that was a princely sum.

And I found out, not from Ty but elsewhere, some other nice things he had done. When Sam Chapman joined the old

Philadelphia Athletics, Cobb took him by the hand and taught him how to play the outfield for Connie Mack.

And while few knew it, when Jackie Jensen decided to quit baseball Ty wrote him a seven-page letter, handwritten, telling him he was making a big mistake leaving the game so young. It had a powerful influence on Jackie and delayed his retirement.

Incidentally, when Ty wired Musial his congratulations on getting hit number three thousand, he wondered who he'd hit his three thousandth off. No newspaper mentioned it in accounts of the game. The Red Sox used three pitchers that day—Joe Wood, Benny Katt, and Herb Thormahlen. Ty wondered which it had been.

"I'd like to think it was Smokey Joe Wood," he sighed. "He'd put his back to you on the mound, then would wheel around and bust one over and you never knew what it was going to be—fastball, curve, or spitter."

Cobb's Pitching "Immortals"

WHAT WERE THE great pitchers of "the good old days" like? No one was better qualified to evaluate them than Ty Cobb, the greatest ball player of all time. The day Big Ed Walsh died I drove down to the Cobb home in Atherton to get Ty's appraisal of the legendary White Sox pitcher.

Were base hits easier to come by in his time? Ty was in his spacious yard trimming rosebushes. He wiped the sweat from his brow with a big red bandana and began.

"Big Ol' Ed. He fought you like a tiger. When the chips were down he was as great as any pitcher who ever lived, today or yesterday. His fastball was a blazer and he put more on his spitter (when it was legal) than anyone who ever threw it.

"He dearly loved to make the hitter think his next pitch was going to be a saliva ball. But I discovered when he actually opened his mouth to apply the slippery elm mixture to it, his cap would go up and down. That was the tip-off.

"But even knowing what was coming you still had to hit it. Once I had a forty-one-game hitting streak going but Big Ed stopped me cold. He'd glare down at you with that icy stare and try to intimidate you. His spitter broke down and his fastball up. He dared you to hit either.

"One season he won forty games. In one stretch he pitched seven out of nine games and wound up hurling both ends of a doubleheader."

We went into the house for dinner and Ty sat me down by

the fireplace to recall Herb Pennock of the Yankees as the greatest left-hander of his time. "He never weighed more than 165 with his socks on," Ty began. "He broke in with the Philadelphia Athletics but didn't last long with them because Connie Mack always preferred big, strapping pitchers like George Earnshaw, Lefty Grove, and Chief Bender to stare a hitter down. So Mr. Mack unloaded Pennock. He was seldom wrong on pitchers, but he surely was on Pennock."

Ty said Herb didn't have blazing speed. There were days when he didn't throw a half-dozen fastballs and those he did throw wouldn't break an egg. And his curve didn't amaze anybody. What he did have was psychology and unerring control.

"Pennock was intelligent and very deliberate. He'd look over every batter before going to work on him.

"He had a way of making the hitter wonder what he was thinking about. Every ball he threw meant something. First time he ever pitched to me he worked the count to three and two. Before winding up for the next pitch he shook off several signs, and I was more puzzled than ever. He had me guessing. I was sure he wouldn't throw me a curve, but that is just what he did—and I struck out."

Ty said it took him a whole season to find out that Pennock shaking off a sign didn't mean a damned thing.

Pennock got to Cooperstown. He deserved it years before he made it. One October he pitched three World Series games in four days. In another he didn't allow a batter to reach first base until the eighth inning. His World Series won and lost record was 5-0. Only Lefty Gomez had a better record in all World Series history—6-0.

One morning I played a round of golf with Ty and Pop Warner on the Stanford course. Pop had coached Chief Bender at the old Carlisle Indian School and was telling Ty that Bender took more books out of the school library than any other student. He was also a crack rifle shot. "He'd go out on the nearby

18

woods and hills for an hour or two and come back with enough grouse over his shoulders to feed the whole school," Pop recalled.

Then Ty gave his evaluation of Bender as a pitcher. "He was the craftiest baseballer I ever knew," Ty began, describing the full-blooded Chippewa Indian born in frostbitten Minnesota.

"Like Pennock, he should have been in the Hall of Fame long before he made it. They waited until he had one foot in the grave before letting him in."

Ty vividly recalled the 1913 World Series. One was out and two on in the eighth inning of a tight game between the Athletics and New York Giants when up to bat came Chief Meyers, also an Indian. "Bender turned his back on Meyers and motioned for his right fielder (one R. Murphy) to move over. Then, with great emphasis, he waved the left fielder (Oldring) to do the same.

"By this time everybody in the ball park 'just knew' Bender was placing his defense so he could throw an outside curve that Meyers wouldn't be able to pull," Ty related. "He couldn't have made it plainer if he had shouted it at the top of his lungs. But instead he wheeled around and threw a fastball right down the slot—a bullet. Meyers was one of the best fastball hitters in baseball but the horsehide was past him before he could get the bat off his shoulder. He had struck out on his favorite pitch."

The Athletics beat the Giants four out of five in that series and Bender won both of his starts. He won six World Series games but he also lost four.

Bender played in an era when Connie Mack had a great pitching staff—Bender, Jack Coombs, and Eddie Plank. Most fans regarded Plank as the big ace. Year after year he won more games than Bender. But take it from Ty, those records were deceptive.

"Mr. Mack," Ty explained, "always matched Bender against

the toughest mound opponents in the league. There were no soft spots for him. He pitched when he'd have to hook up with Big Ed Walsh, Smokey Joe Wood, Walter Johnson, or some other mound giant. Mr. Mack would often pitch him out of turn to win a crucial game.

"Bender was powerfully built, like Allie Reynolds, another Indian, but taller. He had a nice cross fire, a wicked curve, and a ninety-mile-an-hour fastball."

I asked Cobb one day about Walter Johnson, and that really got him started off again about pitchers of his day.

"The Big Train?" he exclaimed. "Gad, how Walter could whistle that fast one through there. Bob Feller, Dazzy Vance, Dizzy Dean? I don't think any of them could match his speed. Nature, when it gave him that lanky frame and those extra long arms that came down to his knees, fashioned the greatest natural fastball pitcher ever. And how he loved to throw it. Any time he shook his head at his catcher (Muddy Ruel) I knew he wanted to come in with another hard one. Harry Heilmann, the great hitter from San Francisco, spent five seasons getting just two hits off him. That's right. Total of two."

Ty paused a moment. A guilty expression and puckish smile seized him. "Y'know," he went on, "he was one of the most decent men in all baseball, any era you mention. He was too much the gentleman to dust a batter off, though I often asked for it. I used to crowd the plate on him. I'd stand up there with my face only inches from it—in fact, my knees were across it and my chin just over the corners.

"I did it knowing Walter with his dangerous speed wouldn't intentionally hit me, though he had every right to. But he was too nice a guy and I knew it. As a result, he pitched me outside and I got many a walk off him. And, believe me, you were glad to settle for a walk or occasionally bunt him for a single."

There was nothing worse than to have to face Johnson on a cloudy day. Ty learned this as a player, but had it impressed on him when he later managed Detroit. In those days the batteries were never announced until about noon of the afternoon game.

"My players would come up to me one by one and beg out of the lineup on hearing the Big Train was going to pitch. 'I've got an awful bad stomachache and I don't think I'd be of much use to you today. I'd like this afternoon off. I'll be okay tomorrow.' It got to be an old story."

Johnson won 420 games lifetime and his club, the Washington Senators, were chronic second divisioners.

Ty said that early in his career, the pitcher who lowered his batting average the most was Addie Joss. "His sidearm delivery was puzzling. He had been around a long time and passed out of the picture before I had a chance to figure him out."

Ty often reminded me that Sherrod Smith of the Cleveland Indians "had the best move to first base" of any pitcher in the game. "He was a wizard at it," Ty said, "but every strength has its weakness. I'd take a short lead on him and bluff my body toward second base after he started his windup. He'd see me out of the corner of the eye and throw a pitchout. This way he'd get in the hole on balls and strikes and often throw a 'cripple' that even a .240 hitter would murder."

Ty said there were a dozen base runners in the majors during his time who were faster than he. "But you don't have to be a Charlie Paddock or Jesse Owens to be a good base stealer. By hours of study and practice I developed a fast break." But Ty's base stealing is another story in itself.

The Bambino and Baltimore

BALTIMORE HAS SUCH historic sites as Fort McHenry, where Francis Scott Key scribbled "The Star-Spangled Banner" on an old envelope as he composed the national anthem in 1814. There is also the house where Edgar Allan Poe composed his classic poem, "The Raven." There's also the unmarked grave site of John Wilkes Booth, President Lincoln's assassin. Baltimore is also where the Orioles demolished the Los Angeles Dodgers, overpowering the peerless Sandy Koufax and Don Drysdale in a four-game sweep of the 1966 World Series.

But to many, the city is remembered as the birthplace and boyhood home of George Herman ("Babe") Ruth, the great home-run slugger. The home where he was born was about to be demolished as a fire hazard when the city fathers decided that it and the Bambino were about as much a part of American life as Robert E. Lee, hot dogs, and apple pie. They bought the house and made it a nonprofit museum, administered by the city recreation and park system.

Thousands of men and women from all over the U.S. come to visit the two-story house at 215 Lester Avenue, where Babe was born in a second-story room on February sixth, 1895, the son of George and Kate Schamberger. In fact, more women than men are said to visit the home where the great Bambino thrived on triple servings of sauerkraut and pig's knuckles, liverwurst and Polish sausage and sundry spreads, all washed down with pails of beer, without ever getting a bellyache.

The bat the Babe used and the ball he sent towering out of the park for his famous 60th homer in 1927 are now in the Cooperstown Hall of Fame, as is the ball he hit for his 714th (and final) homer in the majors in 1935, but the home museum has other intriguing items.

There's a life-size likeness of him autographing balls for a group of idolizing young boys. And there are hundreds of photos on the walls of famous players of his and earlier times—more than are on the walls of Lefty O'Doul's restaurant on Geary Street in San Francisco, across from the St. Francis Hotel—enough to keep visitors to the Ruth Museum occupied for hours if they are true baseball fans.

Eleanor Haby, who was head receptionist and curator at the museum for more than ten years, says the most controversial photo purports to show the Babe pointing at left center field to the spot where he was about to blast a homer in the controversial 1932 World Series against the Chicago Cubs at Wrigley Field. It was a bitterly fought Series in which the Yankees bench, including the Bambino himself, rode the Cubs verbally for voting only half a share of the World Series pelf to Mark Koenig. Koenig was an ex-Yankee who joined the Cubs late in the season, filling in at short in a desperate situation. His play was instrumental to the Cubs winning the National League pennant.

While the feud waxed hot in the fifth inning of the third game at Wrigley, Charlie Root had two strikes on Ruth when the Babe made one of the most brazen, defiant, pantomime gestures in baseball annals by raising a finger and pointing to the Cubs fans who howled in derision.

Was the Babe annoying his tormentors by showing them where he was going to put his homer out of the park, or was he merely telling them, "Look, I've still got one swing left, and it takes only one to hit the long ball"?

Root, first baseman Charley Grimm, and Cubs catcher Gabby Hartnett all swore it was the latter, but the media decided the other version would make a better story. You be the judge. From talking to the sportswriters who covered the game, I'm convinced it was just a coincidence that Ruth pointed a finger in the direction of the very spot his homer went out.

An adjoining house to the one where the Babe was born is used as a small auditorium for showing films and slides of Ruth in the process of compiling some of his fantastic slugging and pitching records. These include smashing 114 homers in two consecutive seasons, hitting 50 or more four different years, blasting 2 or more in one game 72 times, hitting grand slammers twice in consecutive games, hitting 9 homers in one week, 3 homers in a World Series game twice, batting in 170 runs one season, and leading the American League in slugging percentage thirteen seasons. His 714 homers lifetime stood up until Hank Aaron came along forty years later to finally pass him.

There are shots illustrating Ruth getting a homer every 8.5 times at bat lifetime, compiling a .625 batting average in World Series play, and hitting seven homers in five straight games, at least one in each contest.

Ruth's record as a pitcher in Boston is almost as fantastic as his home-run marks. He hurled 9 shutouts in 1916, pitched 29 ⅓ scoreless innings in one World Series (Whitey Ford finally surpassed this), and led the league one season or another in earned run average, games started, complete games, and shutouts.

Current director Michael Gibbons, his assistant, Greg Schwallenberger, and chief caretaker, Steven Spicer, are kept busy answering verbal queries and letters about the Babe's activities on and off the field. They say the two most-asked questions are "Where is he buried?" and "Why did they switch him to the outfield when he was such an astonishing success as a pitcher?"

The answer to the first is that Ruth died August 16, 1948, of throat cancer at the age of only fifty-three, and is buried in the Gate of Heaven Cemetery in New York City. As for the second question, few know the real reason they made him leave the mound for the outfield. It was simply this:

Following the 1919 Chicago Black Sox betting scandal involving players who "threw" the Series to Cincinnati, baseball felt it had to come up with something to erase the memory of the event in the fans' minds or the game would die. A home-run king to make them forget the past seemed a good answer. So the Red Sox sold Ruth to the Yankees for 125,000 shiny Yankee dollars "for the good of the game."

Another feature of the city-administered Ruth Museum is a room dedicated to Baseball's Immortal 500 Club, honoring the twelve sluggers who hit more than 500 in their careers. Besides Ruth and Aaron, there were Willie Mays, Frank Robinson, Harmon Killebrew, Mickey Mantle, Jimmie Foxx, Ted Williams, Ernie Banks, Eddie Mathews, Mel Ott, and, last but not least, Willie McCovey.

In spite of all Ruth did for the game, baseball never paid him more than eighty thousand dollars a year, which was twenty thousand dollars less than Joe DiMaggio got. And Ruth, who wanted to try his hand at managing so badly he could taste it, was never given the chance.

Another sports attraction in Baltimore is the old Baltimore and Ohio depot, where many ancient coaches and steam locomotives are displayed. One is the famous Engine Number 592 that ran on the Jersey Central Line from Philadelphia to New York City. Known as the Speed Queen, she was the first to travel at more than one hundred miles per hour.

Where's the sports angle to this? Well, sir, she made the

record when Arthur Brisbane, a Hearst editorial columnist and executive, chartered it to rush live photos of the first Jack Dempsey vs. Gene Tunney heavyweight championship fight in Philadelphia to the *Journal* and *American* in New York, enabling the papers to make the home edition with action shots.

Colorful Days of Cubs
on Catalina

WHEN HACK WILSON finally made the Cooperstown Hall of Fame, it added a new dimension of interest to Catalina, the island twenty-two miles off the California mainland. A fleet of five seven-hundred-passenger boats, always filled, plies across the channel from Long Beach or San Pedro daily. Catalina looks like a wad of well-chewed gum sticking up out of the ocean from a dim distance. The gum reference fits here, for the island was owned by the Wrigley people for many decades. As the boat approaches shore, the town of Avalon glitters in the sunlight like a polished gem, L.A.'s answer to a South Pacific isle. The shortage and high price of gas has caused California to rediscover Catalina, once the home of such famed dance bands as Jan Garber (until TV came along and claimed them). Visitors are now recalling that the Chicago Cubs, when they were fielding pennant winners, trained here from 1922 (shortly after the island's purchase by William Wrigley, father of the late P. K. and grandfather of Bill.

When I visited Catalina after an absence of over forty years, island officials told me that Wilson's making the Hall of Fame has contributed to the newfound interest in this resort. Tour guides now take their guests up to a canyon about a mile from the Avalon pier, up to the old Cubs park abutting a jewel of a golf course. They show them a spot where the fireplug-built Hack hit what they claim was the longest ball ever cuffed—a 529-foot tape-measure job—from any West Coast ball field.

Lolo Saldama, an Avalon native and the town barber with a shop in the tourist plaza, saw the ball land on Falls Canyon Road. A rabid Cubs fan for years, he remembers retrieving enough long balls, hit by Wilson, Hank Sauer, Gabby Hartnett, and others to keep his team, Avalon High, in horsehides the whole season. "We had a system," he explained. "I'd scramble for a ball the moment it landed outside the park and fire it to a confederate a block away, who, in turn, would throw it another block to another kid working with us. In a matter of seconds the ball would be a couple of blocks away from the Cubs guard and hopelessly out of his reach."

Saldama still feels a little guilty about all the ball thefts because the Cubs used to give the high school all its old uniforms on breaking camp. "And for years, after the Cubs left, Mr. Wrigley leased the Cubs' field to us for only one dollar a year."

Saldama and Duke "Squirrel" D'Arcy, another Catalina semipro, witnessed many legendary training camp episodes. One was when Rogers Hornsby, a hitting perfectionist manager, ordered Hack Wilson to change his batting style right on the heels of Hack's having hit fifty-six homers during the previous (1932) season. Hack heatedly refused.

And there was the tragic sight of Dizzy Dean bringing a full-length mirror to the Catalina Cubs park to better study his pitching style. This was the spring after Diz was hit on the foot by a line drive off of Earl Averill's bat in the annual All-Star game. A broken bone ruined his delivery, and Dean never did make a pitching comeback.

Fans at old Wrigley Field in Los Angeles, where the Pacific Coast League Angels and later the American League California Angels (now at Anaheim) once played, remember the imposing Wrigley Tower, dedicated in 1927 "to those athletes who lost or risked their lives in World War I." The plaque that adorned it is now preserved in a concrete base, just feet from where Hack Wilson's legendary tape-measure long ball landed.

The Wrigleys always went first cabin with their players. They put them up at the swank St. Catherine Hotel or in private cabanas on the island. Late in the 1920s, Cubs players danced at Wrigley's Casino to the strains of Jan Garber's music or that of such other name bands as Ray Noble, Kay Kayser, Freddy Martin, Jimmy Dorsey, and Henry Busse.

Kiki Cuyler was rated the best dancer on the Cubs team. He and Stan Hack were finalists in the annual waltz contest, with Dorothy Lamour, Carole Lombard, Ruby Keeler, Alice Faye, Joan Crawford, or Ethel Merman for partners. Catalina was aglitter with movie stars in those days, with *Rain, Mutiny on the Bounty*, and *Hurricane* being among the films made there.

When Charley Grimm managed the Cubs, he had a "string quartet," with he himself playing a left-handed banjo, Barney Friberg a mandolin, and Cliff Heathcote a ukulele, while Hack Miller (not to be confused with Hack Wilson) strummed a guitar held together with bicycle tape. The "band" often climbed the hill to serenade guests at the Wrigley mansion.

Ed Prell, an ex-*Chicago Tribune* writer, tells me that one year a young rookie radio announcer from station WHO in Des Moines, who did Cubs game recreations there, set up shop in the Catalina press box alongside Warren Brown, Jimmy Burns, et al., much to their annoyance. This young man got Bob Lewis, the Cubs' traveling secretary, to drive him to the dock one morning so he could go take a screen test in Hollywood. He passed it so well he never returned, going on to become a movie star, governor, and president. The young man was Ronald Reagan.

Among the Cubs stars whose faces were familiar on Catalina were Grover Alexander, Guy Bush, Bob Scheffing, Billy Jurges, Pat Malone, Lon Warneke, Riggs Stephenson, and Charlie Root. Root was best known for having been the "victim" of the famed Babe Ruth pointing incident in the 1932 World Series, though he claimed the whole story was "made up" by New York writers.

In 1960 the Cubs had the youngest pitching staff in the majors, and Grimm's first act after replacing Bob Scheffing as manager was to coax Root out of retirement as pitching coach to show how he threw his blazer. I spent a lot of time with Root that spring in Mesa, Arizona, when the Giants were in Phoenix. In 1932 Root, Larry French, and Guy Bush were Cubs pitching mainstays. Lefty O'Doul once told me Root could throw the hardest. Lefty should know. He led the National League that year.

Great Expectorations:
Spitter's Story

ONE SAFE PREDICTION for any baseball season that is certain to hold up is that a new move will be launched to legalize the spitball.

A revival of the saliva ball campaign is overdue. It has been brought up at least every two years since it was first outlawed in 1920, and every time the plea is made to bring it back I think of George Hildebrand, the man who really invented the delivery.

He first used it as an American League pitcher, before becoming an umpire. George guarded his secret zealously until he was about ready to quit playing. Then he passed it along to pitcher Elmer Stricklett, to whom many erroneously give credit for inventing the pitch.

Stricklett also tried to keep the spitter a secret, but it eventually came to be common knowledge and was widely used until banned.

The spitball's greatest exponent was Big Ed Walsh of the Chicago White Sox, Hildebrand claimed; Ty Cobb, who faced Big Ed many times, agreed. However, the Georgia Peach once told us Walsh would have been a great pitcher without it..

Those who had been using the spitter were allowed to continue throwing it because it was their livelihood. Those pitchers included some Pacific Coast Leaguers. We recall Harry Krause of the Oakland Oaks still pitching when his hair was almost white. The spitter had prolonged his career.

Other registered spitball hurlers in the league were Ray Keating and Rudy Kallio of the Sacramento Solons, old Doc Crandall of the Los Angeles Angels, Pudgy Gould of the Seals, and Frank Shellenback.

Frank was the most successful of Pacific Coast League vintage saliva artists. He won 295 games over the years, more than any pitcher in the league's annals. But he was the victim of a cruel error by a White Sox office clerk.

Frank was property of the Sox when the delivery was banned. Those using it had to be registered. The clerk forgot to send his name in to league headquarters and he had to go down to the minors as a result. In later years Shellenback managed San Diego when Ted Williams was breaking in with the Padres, and still later Frank was pitching coach for the San Francisco Giants.

The last registered spitball pitcher in the majors was old Burleigh ("Stubble Beard") Grimes of the Brooklyn Dodgers. He lasted until 1934, when he finally faded out after using the delivery fourteen years after it was banned.

But let me go back to Hildebrand, the true innovator of the spitter. He umpired in the American League twenty-two years after his pitching career ended. He used to drop in at the old San Francisco *Call Bulletin* sports department and, though the spitball had prolonged his pitching career, he was dead set against it, because it was unsanitary. More and more women were becoming baseball fans and they objected to it on these grounds also.

But perhaps the worst thing against the spitball delivery, he said, was that it opened up every deceitful pitch in the book. There were many ways of doctoring the ball, and I guess Hildebrand knew them all.

Great pitchers like Walter Johnson, Christy Mathewson, Chief Bender, and Lefty Grove never needed to resort to trick deliveries. But many others did.

Hildebrand used to cite Dave Danforth of the Detroit Tigers

as the worst offender. Danforth, he claimed, actually knew how to grow warts on the fingers of his pitching hand to make the ball do tricks. He was a chemist by trade, and used to go to sleep at night with his pitching hand in a basin of pickle brine. He'd soak his hand until it was tough as a rhino's hide and grew everything on it but thorns.

As an umpire Hildebrand learned some pitchers would rub talcum powder into the seams of the ball or smear it on the surface. This was hard to detect. It made a fastball hop like a jackrabbit.

Others used Vaseline on the ball, a trick that Gaylord Perry of the Giants and sundry other clubs perfected with much success years later. Another pitcher, whom Hildebrand never did identify, stuck phonograph needles into the ball before making a clutch pitch. It gave the horsehide just the desired pizzazz.

One day in a game Hildebrand was umpiring, a ball Urban Shocker threw was driven crazily into right field. It appeared to be headed out of the park for a homer, but suddenly the cover came off and it came down for an easy out. Hildebrand examined the ball and found thirteen stitches in a row were missing. Shocker had cut the threads with a razor blade.

Hildebrand told me Eddie Cicotte of the White Sox was a paraffin artist. He'd melt paraffin on the side of his glove, then rub the ball over until it was slick. He could make the horsehide do about everything but dance the Charleston..

Others sharpened their belt buckles like the blade of a butcher's knife and then gave the ball a good nick before making a crucial pitch. Still others smeared pine tar in small splotches on the spheroid.

Some used sandpaper to good advantage. They'd sew a little piece of it under their belt, then pull the ball across it. All they needed to do was scuff it up a little, and it would fade away from the hitter.

Pitchers with the Tigers were pretty cute. They'd sew a

cheese grater or fork prongs inside their uniforms. The teeth of these would protrude almost invisibly from the exact place where the ferocious fangs of the Bengal tiger on the insignia were bared. When the pitcher got in a tight spot, he'd just rub the ball, innocent-looking enough, across the chest, nick it, and cause the ball to do the hula across the plate.

So it's small wonder George Hildebrand inveighed against the spitter, calling it a gimmick that would open the way to many forms of cheating and deceit not compatible with the spirit of the game. George was right.

Oeschger's 26-Inning Masterpiece Remembered

AT A RECENT ceremony in Moraga, a plaque honoring Joe Oeschger (pronounced "Eshger"), who went all twenty-six innings in the longest game in major league baseball history, was dedicated on the campus baseball field. Joe, who passed away at the age of ninety-five in the summer of 1986, was the honored guest for the occasion. That memorable game, a 1-1 tie between Joe's old Boston Braves and Brooklyn Dodgers, was played over sixty years ago. Two records that may never be broken in baseball are Joe DiMaggio's fifty-six-game hitting streak and Oeschger's marathon stint on the mound, twenty-six innings.

Can you imagine a manager letting Fernando Valenzuela or Dwight Gooden, for example, risk ruining his arm by pitching just an inning shy of three regulation ball games in one afternoon? Not a chance.

Joe often got fan mail from all over the country from that long contest. He always answered letters, enclosing an autographed mimeographed box score of the game. His rival in that game was Leon Cadore, who passed on about twenty years ago. Joe also came from a long-lived family. His mother was over one hundred when she died.

"I guess if I've been asked once, it has been ten thousand times, if I didn't hurt my arm pitching so long," Joe laughed, recalling the historic contest. But he was able to start, finish, and win a game five days later, and the following season (1921) he was a twenty-game winner.

This, of course, surprised the Boston sportswriters who were his friends, but who had predicted—every last one of them— right after the twenty-six-inning affair, that he'd never pitch again. As Joe explains, the ball was a bit deader in those days. "We were inclined to let them hit it and give our outfielders a chance to earn their pay," he says. "And we didn't take such long warm-ups to start each frame. After the twelfth inning that day, I only threw two warm-up pitches."

There were no lights in parks in those days, and it was getting dark. The players on both clubs wanted the game stopped. They had trouble seeing the ball. Joe wanted to go on, and so did Cadore, but with the contest hopelessly deadlocked and not a run having been scored by either side for the last twenty innings, Umpire Harry McCormick called it due to darkness. The game took only three hours, fifty-one minutes. Lots of nine-inning games take longer today. Nobody kept a count on how many pitches Joe threw this day, but he didn't waste many. He walked only four batters in the twenty-six frames.

Joe compiled an all-time record within a record in this contest. He didn't allow a run after the fifth inning, so went twenty-one scoreless innings in the one afternoon. He remembered each little incident during the long, classic game. "After the fifteenth inning, two of my teammates, Rabbit Maranville and Hank Gowdy, kept cheering me on by telling me in the dugout, 'Joe, go out there and stop them just one more inning and we'll get you a run.' They never did.

"I don't say I wasn't tired after the twenty-six innings," Oeschger volunteered, "but I have been more fatigued in regulation nine-inning affairs. In this long one, there weren't too many tight situations when I had to bear down and pitch my way out of jams. We didn't work on hitters quite as much as they do today. We didn't go for strikeout records, and in this particular game I threw very few curves. My fastball was 'live' so I relied mostly on it."

Joe hadn't known he was going to pitch that day. The Braves' manager, George Stallings, often kept his starter a secret right up until time for batting practice. Today, they know several days in advance if they're going to start. "It rained most of the morning and I didn't think there was much chance of the game being played. But Mr. Stallings had a standing rule that we must report to the clubhouse even if it was pouring.

"Leslie Mann, my roomie, and I had a leisurely breakfast in the old Brunswick Hotel in Boston's Back Bay section, then headed for Braves Field at noon. Our trainer, Jim Neery, gave me a rubdown. This game was played on a Saturday. Stallings liked to pitch me on a Sunday because he was superstitious and played hunches. He liked to start me on a Sabbath because he knew I was a Christian and figured the Good Lord would be on our side.

"But when he posted the lineup in the dugout, there I was, the starting pitcher. I was glad for the assignment because in my last previous start against Brooklyn, I had lost 1-0 in eleven innings to Cadore and I was anxious to even things up. As I say, Stallings was very superstitious. Bats had to be in exact order and kept that way, especially during a rally. The drinking cup had to hang just so on the watercooler spigot. He hated pigeons. Rival players used to torment him by scattering peanuts in front of our dugout, and Stallings would wear our arms out having us throw pebbles at them to chase them away."

Joe was an engineering graduate of St. Mary's. He went right from the campus to the Phillies and became a ten-year man in the majors. After retiring from organized ball, he got a degree at Stanford so he could teach physical education. He taught for twenty-seven years at Portola Junior High in Butchertown, one of San Francisco's poorer sections, where Lefty O'Doul was raised. He turned to physical education because he thought his baseball background was too valuable to throw away.

"I liked working with kids," Joe told us. "My compensation was that I might have helped in a small way to straighten out some of these lads. And when I later saw the success some of them made in life I felt more than repaid."

Joe was that kind of guy.

Joe was once a New York Giant. John McGraw was in desperate need of a good left-hander. He wanted the Braves' Art Nehf (who died fairly recently in Arizona). To get Nehf, McGraw had to give up Oeschger and—guess who?—none other than outfielder Casey Stengel!

An interesting sidelight to the twenty-six-inning game is that a Boston haberdashery firm cleaned up by selling "the longest tie in the world." The necktie had the inning score and the batteries stamped on it.

What did Joe get out of the venture?

"They sent me a free necktie," he laughed.

Taft: First President to Toss Out Opening Pitch

WHO WAS THE most sports-minded president the United States ever had? Americans today are frequently reminded that Ronald Reagan seems almost constantly to have sports on his mind. He was on the telephone talking to Bill Walsh in the Pontiac dressing room less than a minute after the 49ers won the Super Bowl and he hosted the Olympic winners at the White House.

A baseball announcer as a young man in the Midwest, he recreated Chicago Cubs games for the corn-fed listeners of Des Moines, Iowa, where the tall corn grows. Recently he told the Iowa State Legislature, "I've a good notion to recreate the Rose Bowl game for you, and this time Iowa, not Washington, will win." The Hawkeyes got goose egged in the real one—remember?

This isn't all. Reagan's first utterance to Nancy after being shot was, "Honey, I forgot to duck." It was, word for word, what Jack Dempsey told his wife Estelle Taylor, after Gene Tunney beat him for the first time.

Reagan played the legendary Notre Dame halfback George Gipp in the popular Knute Rockne film and also had the role of Grover Cleveland Alexander, the famed St. Louis pitcher, in a film about him.

Sports-minded presidents seem to run to Republicans. Abe Lincoln, the first Grand Old Party (GOP) prexy, was a wrestling filbert. But Demos aren't entirely out of the picture. Franklin Delano Roosevelt (FDR) either loved baseball or had a wise press chief, for he often attended World Series or season-opening games when the Senators were a Washington club. Perhaps it was a bit of both.

Lefty Gomez will tell you one of his big thrills was having FDR shake his hand and congratulate him after a World Series win. And Joe Cronin, another San Francisco Bay Area Sports Hall of Famer, liked to tell of a mad scramble for the ball after Roosevelt made a "wild pitch" to open the 1934 season in Washington.

But William Howard Taft, the GOP standard-bearer 1909–13, was perhaps erroneously labeled the top baseball filbert of the White House, because in 1910 he originated the custom of the president throwing out the first ball for the Senators' opening each year.

It has been said the Cincinnati Reds offered him a contract as a catcher when he was only sixteen, calling for eight hundred dollars a year. Taft's huge bulk surely suggests his position was as a catcher, but his stern father thought baseball was a vulgar game and refused to endorse the contract. Without his signature it was void, because young Taft was a minor.

Richard Nixon was a football bug. Once during a Squaw Valley Winter Olympics conference at which Maxwell Stiles (Los Angeles sportswriter) and myself were the only ones present, Nixon told us he could recite from memory the scores of every Rose Bowl game ever played. This was in 1960.

Ike Eisenhower was a golf-daffy. And he was an end for the West Point Cadets once. An injury kept him from stardom. He liked golf even better than being president. Right after his eight years in the White House I used to see him sitting in the Palm Springs bleachers watching Los Angeles Angels exhibition games in March.

Before becoming president, Warren Harding owned a newspaper and minor league baseball club in organized baseball. This was in Marion, Ohio. Harding is said to be the only president who knew how to keep a box score and how to distinguish an error from a base hit.

Herbert Hoover is said to have played a bit of shortstop at Stanford, and as a senior he was manager of the football team. He was the only U.S. prexy ever to get a Bronx cheer at a ball game. In 1931, with the Great Depression at its height, he went up to Philadelphia to watch Connie Mack's Athletics in a World Series game against the St. Louis Cardinals. He no sooner sat down than the crowd got up and gave him a resounding "Bo-o-o!" One irate fan reportedly yelled, "Two chickens in every pot, eh?" Others cried, "We want beer!" This was during Prohibition (which was given the heave-ho soon as Roosevelt clobbered Herbie in the elections).

Jack Kennedy liked many sports, but his interests were largely focused on participating, not spectating. Gerald Ford was a Michigan Wolverines football star and played center at Kezar Stadium for the East in the 1935 Shrine Game.

Andy Jackson used to like to race his thoroughbred horses and bet on them in match events. Woodrow Wilson failed to make the Princeton baseball nine, but as a senior was manager of the team.

Harry Truman had weak eyes as a kid and wore specs. His friends wouldn't let him play but made him an umpire. He could see well enough to read the racing form and was an avid long-shot bettor in Kansas City when "Bay Meadows Bill" Kyne operated a track there in the early 1920s. At the time, Truman was selling neckties at his own haberdashery.

Calvin Coolidge showed no enthusiasm for baseball. They finally talked him into throwing out the first ball when he was president. It is said this was the only time Conservative Cal ever had a horsehide in his mitts. He left after the third inning, pleading "pressure of official business," a shopworn alibi.

An overlooked sports-minded president was Benjamin Harrison, grandson of William Henry Harrison. Benjamin was the twenty-third president. Recently I read a book called *Lore and Legends of Baseball* by one Mac Davis who claimed Benjamin originated the name *Giants*. He invited a New York club to the White House and exclaimed to reporters, "These fellows are real giants." Davis claims sportswriters henceforth started calling the club "Giants." How it came to be officially named *The Giants*, however, is a different story that can be told some other time.

Lefty
"Goofy like a Fox" Gomez

HE CAME ALONG the sports pike on the final fringe of what is known as the Golden Age of Sports. Vernon "Lefty" Gomez was as San Francisco as cable cars and the Golden Gate Bridge. He was born in nearby Rodeo and signed his first pro contract with the Coast League's San Francisco Seals. As a young baseball writer for the old San Francisco *Call Bulletin* I saw him pitch his first game for them when he was only seventeen.

His debut in 1929 came in a spring exhibitioner against the Pittsburgh Pirates, who in those days trained in Paso Robles. He pitched a three-hitter I'll never forget, nor will I forget his winning of eight straight when league play started. His rise was as meteoric as it was inevitable. Scout Bill Essick of the New York Yankees, who was later to put over the Joe Di-Maggio deal, bought Gomez for thirty-five thousand dollars.

That was big money in those depression days. There were five daily newspapers in San Francisco then, and as the youngest baseball writer in town, it was my fortune to break the story of his sale. It was my first big scoop.

What an exciting pitching delivery Gomez had. It had style and flair. He'd mount the rubber, stride forward, rear back, and fire the ball with a spectacularly high kick. His fastball was a real blazer. Where its force came from is a mystery considering this gangly kid's six-foot-two tall, bony frame that carried only 153 pounds. Ron Guidry today weighs more than Lefty and the Yanks say he is too skinny.

Lefty was to last thirteen years as a pitcher in the majors. His Cooperstown Hall of Fame credentials are indelibly etched in the record books. Most legendary is his unequaled unbeaten 6-0 record, spread over five World Series with wins over such peerless opponents as Carl Hubbell, Lon Warneke, and Dizzy Dean. His best won-and-lost seasons were 21-11, 21-9, 24-7, topped in 1934 with his 26-5 when he led the American League in total wins, most innings pitched, complete games, shutouts, strikeouts, and the lowest earned run average (ERA)—virtually a clean sweep.

And at career's end he was .500 or better won and lost against every club in the league when sluggers on rival teams included Ted Williams, Jimmie Foxx, Hank Greenberg, Charlie Gehringer, and Joe Cronin.

In Lefty's day nicknames in sports were the vogue—the Four Horsemen, the Gas House Gang, the Manassa Mauler, Georgia Peach, Little Miss Poker Face, Dizzy and Daffy Dean. Blessed with a delightful sense of humor, Lefty jokingly told baseball writers his first year in Florida that he was working on an invention of a revolving fishbowl. This prompted Buck O'Neill of the *New York Journal* to anoint him with the moniker *Goofy*. And it stuck. Goofy Gomez. He was goofy like a fox—make it two or three foxes. *Goofy* was a misnomer of the first water.

He married the lovely June O'Dea, a dancing partner of George Murphy's in *Of Thee I Sing* at the Music Box, later leading lady in *No, No, Nanette*, another Broadway hit. It proved one of baseball's soundest and happiest marriages.

His pitching career ended, Lefty had a short fling as manager of the Yankees farm club in upstate Binghamton. On his return to San Francisco after the season ended, I asked where he finished. "In Scranton" was his typical quip.

Lefty became a talented after-dinner speaker for the Wilson

sporting goods people for more than thirty years, a consultant and goodwill man. In that time he has attended 3,427 sports dinners, eaten 3,427 rubber chickens, and told 8,219 funny stories. I never heard him tell the same one twice. And he invariably made himself the goat instead of embarrassing the other fellow.

During his Yankee career, Gomez roomed with half a dozen Yankees, including Babe Ruth and Joe DiMag. His first roomie was the Bambino.

A tale had it that Ruth had a bet going every year with Gomez that Lefty wouldn't get ten base hits all season. "It was five hits, not ten," Gomez was saying, "and the Babe usually won the bet." But it is a matter of record that Gomez banged a hit off Cliff Melton of the Giants that knocked in the winning run of one World Series game.

Once Ruth handed him his own forty-two-ounce bat and said, "Here, kid, use this one and get yourself a homer." Lefty took the big bludgeon into the on-deck circle and made like the Bambino, swinging it lustily. But in trying to knock the dirt off his spikes with it, he hit his ankle and not only went to the hospital for a week, but also lost credit for the win. The Yanks were leading by seven runs when he went out of the game with injuries.

Lefty always gives generous credit to others for his success. "Look at the outfielders I had to shag my fence balls," he said, "—first comes Ruth and Ben Chapman, then Keller, Henrich, and DiMaggio."

When Lefty joined the Seals as a raw rookie, Dutch Ruether, a veteran of four World Series campaigns, took him under his wing and showed him some tricks of the trade. But little Herb Pennock helped him the most, Lefty claimed. This was when I asked him who was the greatest southpaw ever—Grove, Spahn, Koufax, or Gomez?

"None of 'em," Lefty insisted. "In my book it was Pennock. Pennock taught me nearly everything I know about pitching. And Mrs. Pennock was awfully nice to June when we were first married. Herb's curve didn't amaze anybody, and he could scarcely break an egg with his fastball. But he had impeccable control and convinced me of its importance. And he taught me how to psych batters better.

"Dickey would let him shake signs off till the cows came home, but he'd have a fit if I did it. Sometimes Herb didn't decide what to throw until the last second and even Dickey didn't know what was coming. Now there was a great catcher. Dickey had a lot to do with whatever success I had."

Regarding various hitters he had pitched to in his own league, Gomez mentioned Jimmie Foxx, Ted Williams, Joe Cronin, Oscar Melillo, Ethan Allen, Luke Appling, Charlie Gehringer, Hank Greenberg, and Rudy York for openers while over in the National League, in World Series and All-Star games he thought Dick Bartell, Frankie Frisch, Kiki Cuyler, Ernie Lombardi, and Bill Terry were his toughest outs.

For distance, Foxx, Greenberg, and Williams were headaches. "For just plain singles hitting Gehringer could get them off me in a dark tunnel. And Cronin hit me like he owned me. If I'd pitch a six-hitter against his club, three of them would be Joe's."

Bull-penner Johnny Murphy was usually the one who came in to relieve Lefty when he wasn't "right." So when Manager McCarthy one day asked Gomez if he was ready, he got this answer, "You'd better ask Murphy."

Among Lefty's treasured memories is a chat he had with FDR before the second game of the 1936 World Series. The president had decided at the last minute to see the game and his press chief phoned from Washington asking that about 150 seats be set aside for the presidential party. The Polo Grounds were a sellout, but miraculously enough, ticket holders consented to give up their seats for this one game. Lefty beat Hal Schumacher by a horrendous score of 18-4. The Yanks bashed out seventeen hits. Even Lefty got one that day.

Yankee Clipper's 56 Straight

OF ALL THE baseball greats spawned in the San Francisco Bay Area, Joe DiMaggio will live the longest in memories of fans as a symbol of the game. If one word could describe him best, it would be the all-encompassing: class. He had it on and off the field from when he first signed with the old Seals at eighteen, through his brilliant Yankee career, right up to the present.

Joe was seventy years old November 25, 1984. Friends wanted to toss a big birthday party for him in San Francisco, but he nixed it. There was, however, a party of sorts in Atlantic City, New Jersey, on his birthday.

"That one in 1964 was great enough to last a lifetime," he said, referring to the last party when he turned fifty. It was at the Sheraton Palace Garden Court and everybody who was anybody in sports was there, including Mickey Mantle, Willie Mays, Carl Hubbell, Dizzy Dean, and Lefty Gomez, with Mel Allen as emcee.

Joe's hair was turning iron gray then. Now it is nearly snow-white, but he still stands tall and straight and handsome, and he walks down the street with all the poise and dignity that travel, his years in the majors, and a deep sadness in his personal life have bestowed upon him.

Joe was the greatest ball player of his time—Most Valuable Player (MVP), batting champ, American League home-run king—crowns he held with humility. He was on ten winning

Yankees clubs and nine world champions, and there was never a doubt from the first to the last that he was the inspirational source. He was a great power hitter and, like Ty Cobb, could hit for an average as well. His career average was .325. He ran well, threw even better, and played center field best of all.

In the end his number 5 uniform was retired like Ruth's and Gehrig's, and he was voted into Cooperstown in his first year of eligibility—five years after retiring. The last big honor heaped on him was being voted, some years back, baseball's greatest player. Even if one thinks this honor belongs to Mays, Mantle, Musial, Aaron, Koufax, Williams, or Rose, one can't quarrel with it violently.

Born in Martinez, California, in 1914, a few months after World War I broke out, Joe was the eighth child and fourth son of Guiseppe and Rosalie. He was a baby when the family moved to San Francisco and first lived on Russian Hill, just above Fisherman's Wharf where his father, who had emigrated from Sicily, had a boat.

Joe had neither the heart nor stomach to follow in his dad's footsteps. Lefty Gomez once told me he took Joe fishing in Florida. "I had to bait the hook for him and his first cast caught in his jacket. And he got deathly seasick."

Baseball, not fishing, was Joe's game from the start. He learned on playgrounds in North Beach, and also on Funston Field in the Marina. He played semipro for Rossi's and Sunset Produce clubs in a bush league, quit Galileo High to sign with the Seals, and got letters from his dad during spring training reading, "Come home, Joe . . . the fish are running. Give up this game of baseball. It is for loafers."

DiMaggio broke into the Coast League with a rousing triple and a few years later was starring with the Yankees to become the first legitimate one-hundred-thousand dollar–salaried star in the game—receiving twenty thousand dollars more than Ruth ever got.

His fifty-six-game hitting streak was one of the hardest feats to achieve in baseball. No baseball record carries more tension and pressure with each passing day than Joe's streak. Ralph Kiner has given a good answer as to why "Joe's mark will last forever." Forever is a long time, but, as Kiner explained, they strike out more often today going for the long ball. During Joe's streak from May to mid-July, he fanned only seven times. Baseball hasn't changed, but most of today's players aren't content to just meet the ball.

"They also have bull pens now," Kiner reminds, "and are more record-conscious. If a hitter ever gets close to the mark, pitchers will walk him purposely to stop his streak and get an asterisk for it."

Joe's record came amid mounting crises. There were dramatic incidents with humor and pathos. He started his streak by coming out of a bad slump on a balmy May afternoon in Yankee Stadium, avoiding the horse collar by a single in four at bats off Al Smith, Cleveland ace. Nobody paid it much mind at first. Even when it reached twenty the streak got scant mention, a mere paragraph.

But by June 20, he had hit safely in thirty-three straight, passing Rogers Hornsby's best mark. The pressure mounted. Extra snap went into pitchers' curves when he was at bat. All wanted to stop him.

By June 29, he had run his streak to thirty-nine and George Sisler's record was about to be eclipsed. On that day Johnny Babich, a Bay Area phenom developed by the Mission Reds of the Pacific Coast League who had pitched to Joe in the minors, was now with the old Philadelphia Athletics. He walked Joe intentionally twice. The third time, in the seventh, he threw him three straight balls.

Joe, exasperated, looked over to the bench. Manager Joe McCarthy gave him the hit sign. Babich's fourth pitch was a roundhouse curve, outside. Joe lunged, reached across the plate, and got the fat part of the bat on it, smashing a drive through the mound that could have decapitated Babich. It was a clean single.

When DiMaggio singled off the Senators' Dutch Leonard, thirty-one thousand fans exploded. As he came back to the dugout, teammates leaped on him, congratulating the man who had just tied Sisler. Joe sat quietly in the clubhouse between games of his doubleheader, sipped some coffee, and changed his shirt. Now all he needed was a hit in the nightcap to break the magic record, or so he thought. But, lo and behold, the ordeal wouldn't be over. Let Maury Allen in his book, *Where Have You Gone, Joe DiMaggio?*, tell it:

"An amazing story came over the press wires from San Francisco. Jack McDonald, *Call Bulletin* sports editor, had discovered a record topping Sisler's. Wee Willie Keeler of Baltimore had once hit in forty-four straight. So DiMaggio learned he had more games to go to break it. To make matters worse someone stole Joe's favorite bat from the dugout rack between games."

"Your discovery almost made me a nervous wreck," Joe chided the other day, "but I wouldn't want credit for a record I didn't make." Joe tied Keeler's mark in Boston, then, seeking to go ahead and make it forty-five, he faced Bobo Newsom, a right-hander who'd always given him trouble. On his first at bat Joe hit a tremendous blast, but Stan Spence made a circus catch of it. Joe was full of foreboding. He reasoned he didn't figure to hit Bobo that hard again. But his last at bat he whacked a tape-measure homer.

The long hot summer went on. Joe ran his streak to fifty-six, then in Cleveland hit two bullets off Al Smith. Both were shots down the left baseline, which Ken Keltner fielded brilliantly. The last time at bat he hit a hot one down to shortstop;

Lou Boudreau grabbed it and finally shut Joe out of the hit column.

This so unnerved DiMaggio that the very next day he began another streak of seventeen games.

Joe DiMaggio's "Other" Hitting Streak Remembered

THE YEAR 1983 marked the fifty-second anniversary of Joe DiMaggio's sixty-one-game hitting streak in the old Pacific Coast League.

"A while back you wrote a piece about Joe's fifty-six-gamer with the Yankees," reminds Pinky Green, a Hayward reader, "so why not do something on his longer one with the San Francisco Seals?"

Well, why not? In some ways this was a greater feat than the streak he was to have with the Yankees eight years later. Here was a kid either eighteen or barely nineteen, in his first season as a pro, hitting curves like they were going out of style.

Joe faced some good pitching that year. Pacific Coast League mound staffs were comprised of either crafty veterans just down from the majors, some of whom were registered spitball hurlers, or young fireballers on their way up to the big leagues.

I have an old Coast League book giving a chronological recap of Joe's sixty-one-gamer. Among the good ones he had to face to keep his streak alive were Elmer Jacobs, Herman Pillette, spitballer Frank Shellenback, Bobo Newsom, Lefty Vinci, Wee Willie Ludolph, Tom Sheehan, Johnny Babich, Bert Cole, Dutch Lieber, Fay Thomas, and the peerless little southpaw, Tony Freitas.

The sixty-one-game streak started May 28 and stretched

out during the summer, finally ending on July 26. Joe has a vivid recollection of the day he was stopped. For the first time that season the Seals' manager, the late Jimmy "Ike" Caveney of Corte Madera, batted DiMaggio leadoff, figuring it might get him an extra time at bat.

It did. Ed Walsh, Jr., fireballing son of the great White Sox pitcher whom Ty Cobb feared the most at the plate, had stopped Joe cold the first four times at bat. Now it was the ninth inning, the score was tied with one out, and Jack Fenton was on third base.

"Jim Poole was in right field for the Oakland Oaks," Joe recalled. "They pulled the infield in to play for the plate. I hit a long one to right. Poole went way back and made a great one-handed catch."

One-hand catches were rare in those days, used only when a catch could be made that way. These days some outfielders think a two-handed catch is bush league.

Ironically, Joe won the game going hitless because Fenton tagged up and scored easily from third to end the game. The streak was finally ended. It had brought new life to the Coast League, which was struggling at the gate in the height of the Great Depression.

By the time Joe's consecutive hitting streak reached forty, major league scouts flocked to watch DiMaggio. And every pitcher in the league was itching to be the first to stop this red-hot, teenage phenom. One of them was Tom Sheehan, then a pitcher for the Hollywood Twinks but later to become Horace Stoneham's buddy and adviser when the Giants moved to San Francisco.

Sheehan faced Joe in the forty-first game. Tom and catcher Johnny Bassler worked with all the tools and connivance at their command to halt the streak. Joe came into the ninth inning hitless. It was his last chance. Tom got two strikes on him. Bassler than called for three curves. All were balls. Shee-han's curve was off target.

When Bassler signaled for still another, Tom stomped on the rubber like an angry bull, scowled, and thrust out his jaw as he shook the sign off. Bassler came out to the mound. "I was in a sweat," Sheehan recalled. " 'Lookit,' I told him, 'I'm as anx-ious as you to horse-collar this kid, but I ain't going to walk him his last at bat. These fans (Seals Stadium) will roast me alive if I do.' "

Bassler agreed. So Tom fired a fastball up and around the shoulders and DiMaggio rammycackled it for a whistling line drive double to left. "I gotta hand it to Joe," Sheehan told me years later. "He had the guts to lay off the curve and wait for a fastball. And I mean, he really waited. He all but hit it out of Bassler's catcher's mitt."

Joe's streak had other narrow escapes. When it reached fifty, Bobo Newsom bragged in the sports pages he'd "stop this kid." But Joe hit a homer and two singles off him to break Jack Ness's old Pacific Coast League mark of forty-nine. Early in this game Angels Manager Jack Lelivelt ordered DiMaggio intentionally walked, to the derisive boos of Seals fans. In one double-header, Joe didn't get a hit in either game until his last time at bat.

Not until the sixtieth game was one of his hits even ques-tioned. In this one, after going hitless until the ninth, he rapped a grounder to deep short on Sacramento's slow, Bermuda-grass infield. Ray French, a top infielder, couldn't make the play on Joe. Scorers called it a clean hit, but Sacramento fans grumbled.

When going for his sixty-first game, Joe had been stopped four times and it looked as if he wouldn't get to bat again. But the Seals staged a big rally that enabled him to come up in the ninth. This time he hit a line drive single off Lou McEvoy and his streak was still on.

Walsh stopped him in the next game. "He threw me bullets," DiMaggio recalls. "The last time I had faced him I was three-for-five, but (that) day I could do nothing with his blazer."

That season rookie Joe, playing in the country's fastest minor league, smashed 28 homers, knocked in 169 runs, and also led the outfield in assists, with 32.

DiMag Bowed Out with Class

JOE DIMAGGIO BOWED out as a player in 1951, fifteen years after breaking into the majors. He left with grace, poise, and dignity—and also with a resounding double off the New York Giants' ace Larry Jansen in the World Series.

With some writers Joe was reserved, more to avoid saying something he might regret. But with writers from the Bay Area, he felt comfortable and he was more open.

I particularly recall how helpful he was in the 1950 World Series against the Philadelphia Phillies. The Series opened in old Shibe Park; around the batting cage, Joe took pains to explain how, in early October, the sun's shadow fell between the pitcher's mound and home plate, making it difficult to see the ball.

DiMag went hitless in the first game, won 1-0 by the Yankees. The second game developed into a grim pitchers' battle between the Phillies' Robin Roberts and New York's Allie Reynolds. They matched pitches on even terms for nine innings with the score at 1-1.

Pitching duels are nice, but they don't make for exciting reading like home runs do. When Joe came up in the tenth I was wondering what to build a lead around.

DiMaggio made it easy, whacking one into the left-field seats off Roberts. This would make great reading for Joe's Bay Area fans. All during the season the San Francisco *Call Bulletin*'s switchboard lit up like a Christmas tree with callers asking "What'd DiMag do today?"

The following year was to be Joe's last. A heel spur had bothered him ever since he'd been in the army during World War II; he confided it might be his last season, but swore us to secrecy.

He had gone hitless in eleven at bats in the first three games, when in the fourth game, he smashed a two-run homer. In the fifth game he hit two singles and a double, and in the sixth, he again doubled. It was to be his final hit of a great career.

This fine finish made it a good time to call it quits, so in December he announced his retirement after doctors offered him no encouragement that the spur would go away.

"I promised myself long ago I wouldn't try to hang on once I felt the end was in sight," he told me on his return to San Francisco. "I've seen too many beat-up athletes struggle to stay up there beyond their time and it's a saddening sight. I've had my share of injuries and lately they've been too frequent to laugh off. And when baseball ceases to be fun it's no longer a game."

The Yanks wanted him to switch to first base but Joe declined. Five years later he insisted he hadn't regretted his decision and I believe him. He had just turned forty then.

"After all those years in center field I'd be playing first base mostly for my hitting. It wouldn't be me. I wanted to leave the game on top. I wanted the fans to remember me at my very best." That was Joe. And it's the way I remember him. Joe knew when to quit, as he said. Had he hung on, the fans wouldn't be seeing him at his best.

DiMag thinks the 1937 Yankees were the best of his time. This club had Lou Gehrig, Tony Lazzeri, Frankie Crosetti, Myril Hoag, and George Selkirk as regulars, with Red Ruffing, Lefty Gomez, and Johnny Murphy as solid pitchers and Bill Dickey catching. But he thought the 1939 club was a close second. Its personnel was about the same, except Gehrig was gone (replaced by Babe Dahlgren) and Lazzeri had given way to Joe Gordon.

DiMag thinks his best season was his second year as a Yankee when, at the age of twenty-five, he belted 46 homers, knocked in 167 runs and hit .346. But there was surely nothing wrong with his fourth year either, when he hit .381.

Joe found real contentment back in San Francisco, but had some discomfort at first living in New York. There were some difficult years. Never at any time did he burn the candle at both ends, but he did for a time think life on Broadway was an ideal way to live out his span. It proved a lonely life, and Joe was an unhappy man until he decided to come back home to the Golden Gate, where he found true contentment and more genuine friends than he had ever had in New York.

Some friends thought he'd be much happier had he married a nice little Italian girl who could whip up a good spaghetti dinner. He had two tragic marriages, both to blonde actresses. The first was to Dorothy Arnold, who bore him a son; then he married Marilyn Monroe. Joe never looked happier than when he left San Francisco by boat with Marilyn on his honeymoon (accompanied by Lefty O'Doul and his wife, Jean), bound for Japan and Korea. General Douglas MacArthur cited both Joe and Lefty for their work in entertaining U.S. troops during the Korean War.

Joe's marriage to Marilyn proved short-lived. Her untimely death after their separation grieved and depressed him deeply, and for years he carried the torch. The DiMaggios are a close-knit family, and all were happy when Joe came home to stay. Though he attained fame in New York City, he always said "the Bay Area is my real home and always will be."

His unselfishness was a triumph of his character. Always

willing to help others, DiMaggio once flew from San Francisco to Florida at his own expense to help children with heart problems. "I'll go, but no publicity," he said. And he raised thousands for the hospital at a benefit game.

Larsen's Perfect Game

NO WORLD SERIES ever passes without reminding me of Don Larsen's perfect no-hitter—still the only one ever pitched in the Fall Classic. The big, good-natured Californian with a no-windup delivery wrote his name indelibly on the scrolls of Series lore on a bright, Indian-summer day—October 8, 1956—against the old Brooklyn Dodgers at Yankee Stadium.

I never think of that performance without reflecting that, of all the classic pitchers who hurled in the Fall Classic over the years, Larsen was perhaps the most unlikely to pitch a no-hitter. He had been badly cuffed in an earlier start in the Series and had been a playboy off and on all year.

When you think of who would be most likely to hurl a no-hitter in baseball's showcase event, you think of Lefty Grove, Warren Spahn, Christy Mathewson, Chief Bender, Walter Johnson, Sandy Koufax, Billy Pierce, Sal Maglie, Robin Roberts, Allie Reynolds, Harry Brecheen, Red Ruffing, Whitey Ford, Carl Hubbell, Juan Marichal, Bob Gibson, Herb Pennock, and yes, maybe a dozen more before you picture Larsen.

But he did it, and in classical style, setting down twenty-seven straight Brooklyn batters. His control was so nearly perfect that he threw as many as three balls only to one hitter: Pee Wee Reese, in the first inning.

As an added fillip, the San Francisco Bay Area's own Ralph "Babe" Pinelli was the plate umpire that day, and it was the last game the Babe worked as plate umpire. He had confided to me nearly a week earlier that he was going to retire after the series, but pledged me to secrecy as he felt he owed it to Ford Frick, then baseball commissioner. For the final out of the game Pinelli ruled that Dale Mitchell let a third strike go by.

I always liked the way Manager Casey Stengel handled Larsen. He had pitched miserably when he started the second game, allowing four runs in less than two innings before Stengel could get him out. During spring training that year, Don had wrapped his car around a fireplug at three o'clock in the morning. Casey told me later, "Don phoned me before I had a chance to read about it in the papers."

He had that going for him with Ol' Case. "He told me," Stengel went on, "he was just having a little gabfest and a few drinks with the boys and he fell asleep at the wheel goin' home. He was getting patched up at the doc's office when he called me. I told him I was goin' to have to doctor up his paycheck if it happened again and let him off with that warning."

So Stengel got a no-hitter out of happy-go-lucky Don by handling the incident right. Just two days before pitching his no-hitter, Larsen borrowed three hundred dollars on his World Series bonus from the Yankee front office to get him back to San Diego, where he wintered. His no-hitter was worth about one hundred thousand dollars in TV appearances and razor blade commercials later.

After Larsen's no-hitter, a green sportswriter in the clubhouse questioning period asked, "Mr. Stengel, was this the best game Larsen ever pitched for you?" A perfect no-hitter in a World Series would have to be!

That winter when I chatted with Stengel in his Glendale home, he said Larsen was capable of winning twenty games any season if he wanted to do it badly enough, if he set it as a goal and lived up to the determination to do it. "But he was too fond of the bottle," said Casey.

Incidentally, I filed about a one-thousand-word story on the game right after it was played. We had a Morse wire running into the San Francisco *Call Bulletin*, an afternoon newspaper, and because of the three-hour time differential we could make our home edition with a detailed story, box score and all.

I wouldn't trade the experience of watching and writing about the only no-hitter in World Series history, but actually games of this nature aren't as exciting as they are cracked up to be. I struggled writing one thousand words on it, and after several paragraphs, had a deuce of a time to avoid repeating myself. For one thing, there was nothing controversial about the game— that is, there was no play on which an error could be charged, say, instead of being scored as a hit.

Likewise, there was a paucity of fielding gems by the Yankees to help Larsen on his no-hit way. In the fifth inning Mickey Mantle, racing into deep left center, came up with a backhanded catch of a line drive hit by Gil Hodges. But that was about it.

I could have made an issue out of the called strike on Mitchell that ended Larsen's stint for the day. It looked mighty like a ball, but Pinelli, though it appeared he had signaled a strike almost before the ball got to the plate, insisted it was a perfect strike. Anyway, how could you make an issue of it? Larsen had written history, retiring the first twenty-six batters, and only Mitchell stood in the way of his perfect no-hitter. But Dale didn't even take the bat off his shoulder.

Mitchell, incidentally, was pinch-hitting for Sal Maglie, who, in losing by a 2-0 score, had pitched well enough to win under ordinary circumstances—he had held the slugging Yankees to five hits. One was a Mantle home run in the fourth. The other Yank run came in the sixth when Andy Carey singled, was sacrificed to second by a Larsen bunt, and was scored on Hank Bauer's single.

Larsen wound up his baseball career pitching for the San

Francisco Giants. As fate would have it, he was to make three appearances in the 1962 World Series against the Yankees. He relieved in the first three games but pitched only one inning in the first two, and one and a third in the number three game.

His home for years was in San Diego, where he was voted into the city's Sports Hall of Champions.

Wilhelm's Catchers
Also Deserve Credit

THE INDUCTION OF the first knuckleballer in baseball's Hall of Fame poses a problem. And if not a problem, a question: should the hazards of catching Hoyt Wilhelm's famous delivery go unrewarded? Shouldn't the man who caught him be as entitled to enshrinement in Cooperstown as the man who threw it? Some say the catchers are more deserving of a reward than Wilhelm. Perhaps Commissioner Peter Ueberroth, who is notoriously fond of polling fans on the designated hitter and other matters, should include this weighty question.

The man who caught Wilhelm in New York's Polo Grounds was Wes Westrum, well known to Candlestick Park fans as a former coach and manager of the San Francisco Giants. He lives in modest retirement in Mesa. I found him sitting behind home plate during a recent exhibition game and asked how it felt to catch the king of the knuckleballers and first pitcher with that peculiar delivery to be voted into Cooperstown.

Before answering, Westrum showed us the fingers on his right hand. They were as gnarled as a one-hundred-year-old olive tree. The fingers have been broken in about a dozen places.

"A great guy," Wes enthused. "I certainly don't begrudge him the honor they have voted as his. But he put a lot of years on me. I split a finger once in Milwaukee catching him. Look, the scar is still there. I got it taped up and went on catching the rest of the game.

"On days I caught Wilhelm my wife stayed home, and if the game was on TV, she turned the set off. She just couldn't bear to watch."

When asked what the knuckler was like, Wes said, "It used to take off in all directions. Wilhelm didn't know where it was going. I surely didn't either, and neither did the batter. A good nine out of ten of his pitches were knucklers. He was doing the hitter a favor when he made the tenth one a slider or curve."

Sitting alongside was Whitey Lockman, the original San Francisco Giants first baseman. A fellow North Carolinian, Whitey says Cooperstown couldn't honor a nicer guy.

"To be successful with the knuckler a pitcher has got to be a meteorologist and know just how much moisture is in the air, to tell how a knuckleball will react," Lockman said. "The humidity is just one factor in the success or failure of the pitch."

There probably aren't more than a half dozen knuckleball pitchers in the majors today. The two Niekro brothers, Joe and Phil, throw it as well as a sprinkling of others. Why don't more veteran hurlers learn the pitch when their fastball loses its zing? Well, for one thing, it isn't a pitch one can learn overnight.

"You have to start learning to throw it when you're young and keep persevering with it. Confidence plays a big part," says Lockman. "I saw Wilhelm throw it to Ralph Kiner when Ralph was the hottest hitter in the league and the game was on the line at the time, with runners on in the ninth. Kiner struck out."

Although the knuckler carried Wilhelm to the heights of Cooperstown, he doesn't teach the delivery today in the role of minor league pitching coach for the Yankees. Why? "Because you have to be born with the knack of throwing it," he says.

Tom Haller, later the Giants' general manager, also had a taste of catching knucklers in his playing days.

"Wilhelm's really danced," he says. "It fluttered and dropped.

The pitch was surely sweet to Hoyt. It enabled him to pitch until he was about forty-nine. He had a real feel for it.

"The knuckler," Haller added, "is not the kind of pitch to throw in hopes of hitting the corner of the plate for a called strike in a tight situation with runners on."

Actually, the knuckler is old as the hills. It was first thrown before the turn of the century by one Tom "Toad" Ramsey, who used to supplement his income from baseball as an off-season bricklayer. One day he sliced a tendon in the index finger of his pitching hand and found that when it mended, the tip of his finger would not bend straight.

The result proved a blessing in disguise for Ramsey, because the injury resulted in the invention of the knuckler. Ramsey could deliver a ball that had no spin and that would sink in weird, unpredictable patterns.

He mastered the delivery, and one day, pitching for Louisville when the city was in the majors, struck out seventeen Cleveland Indians in nine innings. That season a new rule had been written into the books allowing a hitter four strikes instead of the conventional three. This rule was rescinded after the one-year trial, but Ramsey's fingertip strikeouts became a legend. Indeed, some said he might have fanned all twenty-seven men that day instead of seventeen had he really concentrated on it.

Juan Marichal,
the Dominican Dandy

JUAN MARICHAL, "the Dominican Dandy," was born to pitch. That best describes his classic delivery and career pitching achievements as a Giant, not an old Polo Grounds transplant but strictly a San Francisco development. He has blossomed into as much of a Giants legend as two great moundsmen who preceded him, Christy Mathewson and Carl Hubbell. For most of his fourteen seasons, he was the club's stopper. Whenever he signed for another season, Giant die-hard fans breathed easier, saying "that's another twenty wins in the satchel."

He's still the Giants' all-time leader in most games pitched, complete games, shutouts, strikeouts, innings pitched, and twenty-win seasons (six in all). He was accorded the honor of being the starting pitcher in ten season openers and his number 27 has been retired along with the numbers of four others: Hubbell, Ott, Mays, and McCovey.

He could throw five different pitches with about equal skill and control. Like Fernando Valenzuela, he was an artist with the screwball, but he didn't have to rely on just one pitch. "My fastball wasn't too sharp today," he'd say, and he was telling the truth. So he'd do the job with a curve, slider, scroojie, or change-up. And he mixed them so no batter could wait for any one of his pitches that he might regard a cripple.

The intangible about Juan was that he threw the right pitches at the right time and had impeccable control. He'd retire one batter with his fastball, the next with a curve, and the third

68

with his scroojie. He kept his own book on the league's good hitters by studying their feet. He had them well catalogued. That's why he often shook off his catcher's signal.

Juan was contemporaneous with Sandy Koufax, the storybook lefty. Baseball men have come around to the belief that Marichal was as much the greatest right-hander of his time as Sandy was the dominant southpaw. Juan may not have been quite as quick, but he had more pitches, all of which he threw for strikes. Stan Musial, the great Cardinals hitter, once told me, "When Marichal's fastball is rising it's harder to hit than Koufax's."

Marichal began as a Giant signed sight unseen for a paltry five hundred dollars on the say-so of Dominican scout Horacio Martinez. Juan played shortstop as a boy. He wasn't discovered as a pitcher until he joined the Dominican Air Force as a seventeen-year-old.

His native village was Monte Cristo, far inland from the Dominican metropolis Santo Domingo. This village was in the island's interior, near the Haitian border. There was nobody around to show Juan how best to throw, and he might well have ruined his arm. An older semipro brother showed him only the bare rudiments. When Juan, at eighteen, first reported direct from the Caribbean to the Giants' minor league camp at Sanford, Florida, Carl Hubbell, head man of the farm system, was there, expecting to change Marichal's pitching style at once if there were flaws in the fundamentals. To Carl's amazement, he found none.

Most youths copy some pitcher they see on TV. But there was no TV in Juan's native Monte Cristo. His style was strictly his own.

On the mound, Marichal didn't look like anybody but himself. He learned how to pitch by ear; Hubbell said he threw as if he'd been doing it for years. Above all, Juan had control. Most pitchers learn it the hard way, but Marichal had it from the start. Hubbell had spent five years in the minors mastering control—ditto Warren Spahn. Jack Sanford was seven years getting to the majors due to wildness.

The first thing a writer noticed about Marichal's pitching was his stats showing a ratio of about four strikeouts to every base on balls, a ratio he was to maintain throughout most of his career. Juan spent a season with an Indiana club in Class D, and a second with Springfield in the Class A Eastern League, where he showed enough speed and control to qualify for the majors.

But the Giants decided he'd benefit by a season with the Triple A Tacoma club in the Coast League, a Giants farm. In mid-season a crisis developed on the Giants' pitching staff so they brought the Dominican Dandy up to the big tent. Less than forty-eight hours after donning his first Giants uniform and after only two seasons in the minors, Juan was started July 19 against the Phils at Candlestick.

His debut was spectacular. First off, he showed an exceptionally high delivery kick à la Lefty Gomez and Dazzy Vance— not as smooth a one, but higher. Juan's had an explosive flair. He virtually threw his legs and hips at the hitters so they didn't get a good look at the ball until it was right upon them.

He struck out twelve Phils that day, beating them 1-0 and allowing only one hit. He had a no-hitter going until pinch hitter Clay Dalrymple hit a slow curve for a cheap single in the eighth. Four days later, Juan proved his debut was no fluke by beating the Pirates 3-1. Then the old Milwaukee Braves came to town and Marichal up and beat the great Warren Spahn 3-2. Juan was barely old enough to vote, and had been only nine years old when Spahnie had his first twenty-win season.

There was a great to-do in this game when the Braves protested that Marichal had one foot three feet to the right of the rubber when he took his first step to pitch. Plate Umpire Jocko

Conlan ruled it legal, and Juan showed his poise by disposing of the next ten hitters after the complaint.

Braves' pitcher Lew Burdette was skeptical. "I've seen rookies break in with all that stuff and they're back in the minors now; wait till he has been around the circuit the second time," he warned. This was the conventional approach to a pitcher making such an explosive start.

But the Dominican Dandy kept right on winning, and was to do it for thirteen more years. Season after season he was the Giants' stopper and manager's meal ticket, just as Sal Maglie had been in the old Polo Grounds days. Every time Juan signed a new contract, fans asked each other, "Where would the Giants be without Marichal?" The answer was, for the most part, "In the soup."

The year 1963 was Juan's crème de la crème season. He was the only Giants pitcher to hold up his end following the club's 1962 pennant year. Juan led the staff in five departments: most wins (25), complete games (18), strikeouts (248—third in Giants history), ERAs; and innings pitched (most in either league).

His feats that year included a no-hitter and a 1-0 win over Spahn, which Manager Alvin Dark called the greatest pitchers' duel he had ever watched. Spahn made only one bad pitch—a home-run ball to Mays in the sixteenth. Marichal threw 227 pitches, 27 more than Spahn, but finished stronger.

His no-hitter, against Houston at Candlestick, saw twenty-nine batters facing him. He only walked two. Only hard-hit ball was by Carl Warwick, a wicked line drive that McCovey speared. It was like the fabled smash of McCovey into Yankees Bobby Richardson's glove in the 1962 World Series. In the ninth, only three outs away, Juan showed his class by striking out Brock Davis and Pete Runnels and getting Johnny Temple to pop up.

Marichal's 1963 pitching record could have been mistaken

for Koufax's. Each won twenty-five. Koufax had forty-one starts, one more than Juan. They were noses apart in everything but strikeouts. Sandy had 304, Juan 248.

Koufax pitched a no-hitter that year to beat Marichal, but Juan came back a few weeks later to beat him with a four-hitter. Spahn said at season's end Juan had a wider variety of stuff than any pitcher in the game; the Giants' Tom Sheehan added, "He isn't afraid to put any of his pitches over the plate. He won't beat himself by walking a man." In one 1963 game Juan made only ninety-five pitches.

One incident blurred his great career. He had a run-in with Catcher Johnny Roseboro of the Dodgers, hitting him over the head with his bat at home plate. This was surprising because of Marichal's even, amiable disposition. He had the gift of easy laughter, a smile as gay as his native Caribbean on a sunny day, and took a cheery view of things. His act was attributed to a sudden burst of Latin temperament; he got off with a long suspension and big fine.

Juan never had serious arm trouble. It led Giants trainers to speculate that there must be something in the muscle structure of Latin Americans that makes their arms more elastic. In Juan's case, his sore-proof arm is even more amazing because for years he pitched virtually year-round. Soon as the National League race was over, he would head for his native country and pitch all winter in the Caribbean League. "I pitch in the winter so my countrymen will not get angry with me," he said, but it was actually a case of "no pitch, no passport" (back to the United States in the spring).

A word more about Juan's explosive high kick. It helped his coordination. He'd come down, landing slightly off balance following his delivery. The Giants feared he might get seriously hurt from a batted ball. He landed slightly to the left of the mound, and consequently a few balls got through for cheap hits. This high kick required tremendous expense of energy, but Juan pitched over long stretches with only three days' rest instead of four.

His favorite hobby was spearfishing for barracuda in the Caribbean. He operated sixty feet deep and once told me, "Barracuda do everything you do. If you advance, they advance. If you back up, they back up. Sharks? They kill a few every year, but I'm not afraid—just careful."

Marichal is happily married to Alma Rose, a childhood sweetheart.

Greatest Lefty Hitter:
Ted Williams

WHO WAS THE best left-hand hitter of all time? This is a rather large question. I asked Casey Stengel and he said, "I can only speak of the last thirty years in which I was around. It would hafta be Ted Williams." Ol' Case told us this on the eve of Ted's installation in baseball's Hall of Fame in Cooperstown. Ted didn't poll a unanimous vote, but few ever have.

"Them as voted against Williams must have been pitchers," Stengel cackled over the phone from his Glendale home. "If he depended on them to get him into Cooperstown he'd be waitin' out in the snow for years."

Going behind Ted's bare "statisticals," as Casey called them (Williams hit .406 in 1941 as the last one to attain the .400 plateau), he was six times American League batting champion and third on the all-time home-run list at the time (behind Ruth and Jimmie Foxx). Stengel called Ted the greatest left-hand hitter in the last thirty years.

"He wore pitchers out," Ol' Case offered. "When I had the Yankees I never knew him to waste a time at bat. I hafta say he was a tall man with a large strike zone and nobody ever had better judgment at picking out a pitch. I never saw anyone who could check a swing quicker and it cost many a pitcher a ball count. That's why they all hated his guts."

Ol' Case said he could go way back and possibly take in better lefty hitters—back to Cobb and Speaker, later Paul Waner or Frank O'Doul. "But if I looked 'em all over for hitting purposes, either for an average or as a slugger, I'd hafta say he was the best of his time."

Stengel paused, as if to run them over in his mind's eye, thinking doubtless of Stan Musial, Enos Slaughter, Duke Snider, Yogi Berra, and Johnny Mize. "Now if I wanted a guy who could do everything, why, maybe Stan is my man over in the National League. But if I'm lookin' for someone to swing the bat, it's Williams. Not that he was a bad fielder. He could stop the runner from taking another base.

"Williams was the greatest left-hander of his time, just as Joe DiMaggio was the best right-hander. Now if I'm looking for a guy with power to either field, I might take Yogi Berra, though he wasn't as sure a hitter. Yet he was amazin' at hitting for distance either to right or left."

I also asked Lefty O'Doul, who said, "Ted had a perfect swing and perfect balance and something else. He was fearless at the plate. I can name a dozen potential Ted Williamses, just as gifted, but they were gun-shy. Good hitters aren't afraid, no matter who's pitching."

Lefty Gomez said he helped Ted make the Hall of Fame. "He hit at least twenty homers off me. He'd come to bat and yell out to the mound, 'How's the family, Lefty?' And before I could answer he'd be on third with a triple."

Cookie Lavagetto said, "When I managed Washington, I never figured a way to stop Ted. Home plate is seventeen inches across, and if a ball was a sixteenth of an inch outside, he'd just look at it. The umpires didn't give him the best of it, but they never got careless with their calls either, because they knew there wasn't a hitter in all the game with better eyes and depth perception. I'd bring in a left-hander, Hal Woodeshick or Mickey McDermott, to pitch to him, but he'd hit them as good as right-handers."

I had many a bull session with Ted in and out of season. I also met him when his marine four-motored navy plane put down at Moffett Field, down on the San Francisco Peninsula, after his hitch in Korea, where he had flown thirty-nine combat missions. Ted went from the field to Oak Knoll Hospital, where he was being discharged for defective hearing.

"Maybe I can't hear the fans boo me now," he joked. "But there's nothing wrong with my eyes."

Tests taken by the marines when he went back in the service showed him to have a depth perception shared by only five out of every one hundred thousand people! Ted had had to make a comeback once before, but he'd been in a different age bracket then. "I was only twenty-seven when I got out of World War II," he reminded me. Now he was thirty-five. "Ruth was still hitting homers at that age," he said, confidently.

As had been the case with another great hitter before him, Rogers Hornsby, one of Ted's big assets was his eyesight. Hornsby wouldn't smoke or drink, and even shunned movies for fear they might impair his vision at the plate. He never put on glasses until he was sixty-one, and then only to read. I once asked Hornsby what was the most important prerequisite for a good hitter. Without hesitation he replied, "Not being scared up there at the plate, no matter who's pitching."

And who was the greatest hitter in baseball today? This was 1958, while Hornsby was a coach with the Cubs, then in training at Mesa, Arizona. "I must say Ted Williams. But if I wanted someone who could play every day and be a team man, it'd be Musial."

While Ted was still active in player ranks I asked if there'd ever be another .400 hitter in the majors. "Sure," he said. "Somebody will climb up there again. Why, when I was an old man thirty-nine years of age I hit .388, and that's only six base hits away from .400 for a season. But a lot depends on who is hitting around you in the batting order. I had Joe Cronin and Jimmie Foxx one year, then Rudy York and Bobby Doerr. But my big break was when Vern Stephens followed me to the plate. They didn't walk me to get at him because he was too tough an out."

Though Williams and DiMag played in the other league, Ralph Kiner, the Pittsburgh Pirates home-run slugger, called them the two best hitters of their time. He was the perennial homer king of the National League for many seasons, and is credited with making the classic remark, "Homerun hitters drive Cadillacs, singles hitters jalopies." Ralph claims he never said it. The quote was attributed to him in a national magazine, but the originator was one Fritz Ostermueller, a Pirates pitcher.

Kiner said if home runs were everything in hitting, both Joe and Ted were playing in the wrong ballparks. "If Williams wore a Yankees uniform, he would have hit more than sixty homers a year, and so would DiMaggio if he played in old Ebbetts Field, Brooklyn.

"Sure, I went for homers," Kiner told me. "I set my stance for them and they were mighty good to me. My lifetime average in the majors was only .280, but if I had hit .400 every year it wouldn't have put as much on my paycheck as 1952, when I hit fifty-six homers and another I lost because it rained before the fifth inning and didn't count."

After those fifty-six he was paid ninety thousand dollars. "I went for homers because it helped me, but also my club. A foolish mistake so many make is trying to sock home runs when they aren't physically built for it. You need a powerful physique, like Ted Kluszewski, Duke Snider, or Eddie Mathews to hit forty or more in a season."

Ferris Fain, who hit his way to the majors as a San Francisco Seal, took umbrage at Kiner's remark that singles hitters drive old Model T Fords. "I drive a Cadillac," he mentioned. "If they paid off on my home-run production when I led the league in hitting two seasons, I'd be driving a jalopy. I hit only two in 1951 and three in 1952."

Fain had just signed a White Sox contract calling for thirty thousand dollars a year—big money then. "In Kiner's case, home runs were money in the bank, but in my case, the most I hit in one season was ten—and when I did, my average fell to .260, an all-time low for me. So I went for singles, and it paid off with two successive league batting crowns."

Bob Feller:
The Real Strikeout King

ONE OF THE real overhyped duels was baseball's strikeout battle—Houston's Nolan Ryan vs. Philadelphia's Steve Carlton for the all-time lead.

As the 1985 curtain rose, they were only 2 strikeouts apart—Ryan leading with 3,874. The hype artists would have you believe Carlton is breathing down the leader's neck, but the duel shouldn't even be close, for Ryan is a younger man and will last longer. He may have lost a few miles per hour off his fastball, but he is still good for 9 or 10 strikeouts per game.

But the reason I can't get excited over the current Ryan-Carlton thing is that, in my book, Bob Feller is the uncrowned king of the strikeout artists. Blazing Bob (or Rapid Robert) suffered more from being in the armed forces during World War II than anybody, including Ted Williams. Feller didn't even wait to be drafted. He enlisted right after Pearl Harbor. The navy kept him in for four years, and he didn't serve his hitch playing service ball, either. He was an antiaircraft gunner on the battleship *Alabama* and was in eight major Pacific campaigns.

The years he missed were potentially the best of his career. He was in from age twenty-three to twenty-seven and didn't get out until after V-J Day, though he surely had enough overseas points to merit an earlier discharge. Those are the big years for a pitcher.

Johnny Vander Meer hurled his consecutive no-hitters when

he was twenty-three, Rube Marquard won nineteen straight when he was twenty-two. Walter Johnson, Christy Mathewson, Cy Young, and Denny McLain all had thirty-victory seasons in that age group, and Don Larsen pitched his perfect game in the World Series at twenty-seven.

Yes, those were prime years Feller lost. Once he said that he thought it had cost him perhaps 1,200 strikeouts. He fanned 261 the season he left and 348 his first full season back, when he was generally considered the best pitcher in either league.

Garry Schumacher, veteran Giants publicist of years past, used to say great pitchers could be divided into early and late bloomers. Lefty Grove, Grover Alexander, Bob Gibson, and Sandy Koufax were all late bloomers.

Feller was surely an early bird. I recall listening to Cy Salpnicka, one of the great all-time scouts, tell how he signed Bob off an Iowa farm for a relatively small bonus. A few years prior to that, Cy bought Earl Averill from the Seals for sixty thousand dollars.

Bob signed at seventeen. That spring he pitched a lot against the New York Giants as they played exhibition games across the South against the Indians.

In his first big-league start, Bob fanned fifteen bewildered St. Louis Browns. In his next start, he struck out seventeen batters against Connie Mack's Philadelphia club, breaking Dizzy Dean's single-game mark. Feller's top strikeout effort was eighteen. Carlton broke it years later with nineteen.

By the time Feller was old enough to vote, he had won 55 games. Before his twenty-third birthday, he had fanned 933—220 more than the next best total at the same age, Johnson's 707.

As mentioned earlier, Feller struck out 348 batters his first year back from the war. The record at the time was said to be Rube Waddell's 343. Late in the season, with his club going nowhere, Bob decided to go for that mark. The Wheaties people offered him five thousand dollars if he did it. Feller wrote the league office, asking what the existing record was. He was told it was 343. Later, after he had finished with 348 strike-outs, the league office advised him that Waddell's record was 349—1 more than Feller had achieved. Wheaties paid off anyway.

He Saw Willie First

MANY MAJOR LEAGUE stars owe their careers to the alertness of California-based scouts. Among these ivory hunters was Eddie Montague, a product of San Francisco's Golden Gate Park and the city's sandlots. He was the "discoverer" of Willie Mays, having seen him first in the wilds of Alabama when he was a virtual unknown save for a handful of Birmingham Barons fans, a club in a league of blacks. The story of Mays's discovery has been told only in bits and pieces. It is one of the real, all-time scouting sagas.

In June, 1950, Eddie got a wire from the New York Giants' front office to mosey down to Birmingham and take a look at a first baseman named Alonzo Perry of the Barons. Montague looked at Perry, but not for long. For out in center field was an eighteen-year-old boy just out of high school—Willie Howard Mays (the first name is Willie—not William).

The first thing to catch Montague's eye was Mays's arm, perhaps the least-publicized thing in the superstar's bag of skills—hitting, fielding, and running being considered tops. "I had seen Yankee Bob Meusel play and his throwing arm was one of the best," Montague told me. "But Mays's was just as good. The first time I saw him come up to hit, he whacked a long homer. He had quick hands, the kind Joe Louis possessed in his time."

Eddie hardly took his eyes off Mays during that Sunday doubleheader. "I watched him from the grandstand roof and some of the things I saw him do were so amazing I almost fell off!"

To make sure his eyes weren't deceiving him, Montague followed the Barons to Tuscaloosa the next day. He had to work quickly because Ray Blades, the Brooklyn Dodgers scout, was hanging around, as were some bird dogs representing the Braves, Indians, and Red Sox. "But they were all dickering with a fellow named Hayes, who owned the Barons," Eddie said. "A friend tipped me off that Mays wasn't under contract to the Barons. After the game I asked Willie about this and he told me he was a free agent."

That night Eddie phoned Horace Stoneham, owner of the Giants. "But what about Perry?" Horace asked, rather peevishly. Eddie told the boss to "forget about Perry," saying Mays was a real find.

"How good is he?" Horace asked.

"Good enough to be just the best center fielder in baseball in another year," Montague replied. Reluctantly, the Giants authorized Montague to pay Willie a bonus of four thousand dollars and give him a contract calling for two hundred fifty dollars monthly to play with Trenton, a Giants farm club.

Willie, the oldest of eight or nine children, lived with his aunt and father, who signed the papers for Willie, who in turn swore he was not under contract to the Barons. Four scouts were dickering for Mays when they found out Montague had just signed him. Just to make sure the Barons couldn't claim to have any strings on Willie, the Giants paid the club ten thousand dollars for a written clearance.

Perry, the man Montague was rushed to Birmingham to sign, vanished into oblivion, while Eddie's prediction that Mays would make the majors quickly proved justified. He came up to the Giants' main club after ninety games with Trenton and forty-two with Minneapolis, then in the American Association.

Tommy Heath, who was later to manage the San Francisco

Seals, takes up the story here. "They sent Mays to me at the start of the 1951 season," he began. "At first I didn't know just where to play him. We had a fine center fielder, Johnny Knopf, who had played the season before and had helped me win the pennant. I sat Willie on the bench in our first exhibition game. He was crestfallen—thought he wasn't going to make the club.

"The next game I put him in left field in the third inning. The ballpark in Sanford, Florida, where we trained was an old tumbledown thing, and the first fly ball that came out to Willie he chased right through the fence, knocking the boards out. But he hung onto the ball, and he got three hits in four at bats, all for extra bases."

The following day Heath started Willie in center and played him every inning of the remaining twenty-five exhibitions, plus the first forty-two of the regular season, when the Giants called him up at Manager Leo Durocher's insistence. Mays was hitting .447 at the time for Minneapolis. After about a week in the American Association, pitchers had Mays hitting the dirt. And they didn't throw just to brush him off. All over the loop they knocked him down, but eventually they had to get the ball over—and when they did, he belted it out of the park. He was so sensational Durocher felt impelled to send for him.

Pitchers on the Giants' staff helped. They had been impressed with Willie in Florida exhibitions that spring and saw a chance to win the 1951 pennant with him. The Giants did win it. But Durocher had to talk turkey to the front office, asking why his club should be handicapped for lack of a center fielder when it had the country's best right in their farm system.

The telegram ordering Mays to join the Giants in Philadelphia at once was sent to Sioux City, Iowa, where Minneapolis had an in-season exhibition game scheduled. Heath chased all over town looking for Willie, finally finding him about midnight, sound asleep in a movie theatre. He caught the plane East just in time.

The story of Mays's early days with the Giants is better known. In his first batting practice he hit the first four pitches out of the park, but then went twenty-one at bats without a hit. When he finally connected it was a good one—a homer off the great Warren Spahn, then in his prime.

Montague was not the only alert California scout. There was Bobby Mattick, whose big find was Frank Robinson of Oakland, but who also signed Vada Pinson, Curt Flood, and Jim Maloney. Then there was Bill Essick, who signed Joe DiMaggio off the Seals for the Yankees.

But perhaps the greatest of the California scouts was Joe Devine. Working for the Pirates and later the Yankees, he was either directly or indirectly responsible for the discovery of Dick Bartell, Wiz Kremer, Larry French, Jerry Coleman, Billy Martin, Paul Waner, and Jackie Jensen.

Devine got only $175 a month as a full-time Pirates scout. His first big find was Kremer, but Owner Barney Dreyfus balked at the price because Wiz was twenty-nine years old. "But he'll win for you," pleaded Devine.

"Okay," said Dreyfus, "but he flops, you're fired." Joe wasn't fired. Kremer pitched the Pirates into a World Series.

A dozen big-league scouts looked Paul Waner over and walked away. But Devine went after the Ada, Oklahoma, kid who became one of the great all-time hitters with a .345 average as a Pirate for ten years.

No sandlot or college diamond was too far away for Joe to visit in quest of talent, and once convinced an athlete had it, he pursued him until he signed him.

Without a doubt, the scout who had the hardest luck of any working on the Pacific Coast (or anywhere in America, for that matter) was Freddie Hoffman, scout for the old St. Louis

Browns. Through no fault of his own, he missed out on three of the greatest: Joe DiMaggio, Yogi Berra, and Mickey Mantle. Could anyone top this?

In 1932 when DiMag, a sandlot shortstop at the time, showed up at Seals Stadium, Hoffman thought he looked great. He signed Eddie Joost, Babe Dahlgren, and Walt Judnich for $125 a month. "I offered Joe the same but he balked, wanted $150. My front office said no. Next time I saw DiMag he was wearing a San Francisco Seals uniform."

In 1942 the Cardinals gave Joe Garagiola $600 to sign. "But I liked a pal of his, Yogi Berra, better," Freddie said. "My boss, Bill DeWitt, wouldn't go any higher than $500, and Yogi's pride demanded he get what his friend Garagiola got. DeWitt finally came up to $550, but Yogi said no dice, so I lost out again.

"The minute I saw Mantle, I wanted him. This was when he came to St. Louis, in June, 1949, and asked for a tryout. He was only seventeen and his arms and shoulders made my eyes pop. I knew he must have power.

"Before I could get him in a suit it started to rain. After a long wait it was still pouring, so I gave him meal money and told him to come back next day. He did, but it rained again. It stopped, but the umps wouldn't let anyone work out on the slippery field. So Mickey went home to Oklahoma and finally popped up in a Yankees uniform for a small bonus and $175 a month. Can you beat it?"

Frankly, I can't.

Mays Woos and Wows SF

WILLIE MAYS OR Joe DiMaggio? One can always stir up arguments over which center fielder was better. The story of Mays's beginning as a New York Giant is well known. Not so well known, though, is the story of Willie's many heartaches when he first came to San Francisco, trying to win full acceptance from Bay Area fans.

It wasn't easy. He was performing before a critical audience in his maiden season on the Coast (1958). Most of the fans watching him had also watched DiMag, the perfectionist, play center field at this same Seals Stadium his rookie year. Joe set a high standard of play, but even the most exacting critic would have to concede Mays measured up his first season in San Francisco.

He came to town amid a tremendous buildup in the press, for he was the only star on the Giants roster and the front office did all it could to exploit him to the fullest for the box office value. Indeed, he was showcase stuff in his fine 1958 season: he hit .347 (then his major league high), led the National League in runs batted in (RBIs) with 121, while his hits—208—were more than he'd ever made.

But there were still many pockets of fan resistance. Some San Francisco fans regarded Orlando Cepeda as their guy. The Baby Bull had begun his big-league career that season. He was no Polo Grounds transplant à la Mays. Fans tolerated Cepeda's shortcomings but demanded perfection from Mays's every move.

Those who'd seen DiMag achieve stardom before their very eyes refused for a long time to put Willie in the Yankee Clipper's class.

Looking back on it after several years in a San Francisco uniform, Mays told me, "I can understand the fans' reluctance to accept me. This is Joe's hometown. He's their idol. He was mine, too. I used to go over to Yankee Stadium to see him play when I was with Trenton and had a day off. This was before the Giants brought me up. I didn't come to San Francisco to show Joe up. I only wanted to prove that I, too, could play baseball."

To this day, some San Francisco fans consider it a sacrilege to call Mays greater, or (for some) even to put him in the same class. Even before seeing Mays I'd concluded that, except for the 1954 World Series against Cleveland, from the records he was close to perfect as an all-around ball player. Find me another player who hits for an average, smashes homers, runs, throws, and fields exceptionally well, too. After all, what else is there to judge a player by?

With some fine players, there's usually one of these skills lacking, but Mays seemed to have them all. Ty Cobb was not a power hitter, nor did he have a strong arm. Mickey Mantle came close. But Mantle didn't field as well or throw with Willie. Mickey had more power than Mays in that he hit the ball farther, but it doesn't show up in his total homers and extra base hits. Mantle could run as fast as Willie, yet he wasn't the instinctive base runner.

DiMag put everything into the record book that Mays did except stolen bases, because the Yankees played a different style of game, going for the "big inning" rather than running. They had a power club. Joe was a great fielder, even superior to Mays, and we've heard players say they'd go to their grave thinking DiMaggio was the best of them all for style.

Yet you hear guys like Tommy Henrich, who was a teammate of Joe's, say the catch Willie made in Pittsburgh in 1956 was the greatest he ever saw in his life, and that there was no equal to the Say Hey Kid when it came to scoring from first base on a double.

Casey Stengel once gave me a comparison of the two, without my even prodding him to do it. "Now, if you was to ask me which is the better, Mays or DiMaggio, I'd hafta say it is hard to tell, because they didn't hit against the same pitchers," he began. "Put Mays in there at Candlestick where the wind blows a gale and he makes catches for the whole outfield. He's great on fly balls hard to judge in that wind. I seen him play in the All-Star game there and other outfielders were awestruck by it.

"As for the hitting, I think the National League has stronger pitching. In the American they'll claim that ain't true, but it is. But there were guys like Bob Feller in Joe's time and he was hitting against better pitching than they had in the National. Mays and DiMaggio are superstars who did it all their life. Their 'ordinary' years were better than some stars' best ones.

"Of some they'll say 'He was great but he couldn't throw' or 'He could do everything but go to his left,' and they both hit for distance consistently. I don't think either of 'em were weak for fielding, running, throwing, or hitting. You name it and they had it.

"Mays out there where the wind was blowing made all the catches, and if you had to have a stolen base, there he was. And he doesn't fall down going from first to third on a single. I'd have to say both could beat you so many ways."

Willie's home-run power always amazed me. He was perhaps the "littlest" of the big home-run hitters, the smallest of those greats who dominated with homers, including such behemoths and near-behemoths as Ruth, Gehrig, Mantle, Williams, Hack Wilson, Ralph Kiner, Eddie Mathews, Hank Greenberg, Ted Kluszewski, Johnny Mize, Willie McCovey, and even Stan Musial.

Mays, at five foot ten, was small in size among the top fence busters. And during most of his career he stayed between about 180 and 187 pounds. Unlike Hank Aaron, whose power was in his wrists, Mays was a swinger who generated his power from the biceps and shoulder muscles.

Considered among others in the upper brackets of the homer hitters, Willie was perhaps the smallest—make it "least big." Ruth was spindle-legged but had weight, girth, and big arms and shoulders. He weighed about 225. Gehrig, though played in the movie *Pride of the Yankees* by skinny Gary Cooper (a tall string bean), was a big man, a husky former fullback, over six feet tall and weighing around 220. Jimmie Foxx was a big bulky guy, all muscles, like Ted Kluszewski. Musial wasn't very tall but was a solid 210. Mize, a big, towering guy, was husky and built on the order of Orlando Cepeda. DiMaggio was well put together. He weighed around 195 as a player and that made him a bit heavier than Mays. Hack Wilson was a short, squat fireplug weighing well over 200. Kiner had a big frame, and while you couldn't call him a Ruth or Gehrig for size, he weighed about 205. The great homer hitter contemporaneous with Mays was Aaron, who weighed about 185. A good ten years before Aaron became the numerical number one total homer hitter of all time, Mays predicted Hank's becoming the one to top Ruth.

The phrase "He can beat you so many ways" was uttered a million times about Mays, even before the Giants first set foot on San Francisco. Many Bay Area fans gagged on it. They were the types who, if Willie didn't make at least one circus catch or hit one homer a game, didn't regard him as super.

But there were few disbelievers at Candlestick on Memorial Day, 1960, in a doubleheader. It was Willie's best day in a San

Francisco uniform and I cite it as a sample of how many ways he can beat you.

His catch of Ed Bouchee's line drive in deep right center started things off. He had to race for a ball drifting away in the high wind. Then came a two-run homer over the left field wall. But his big play might have been scoring all the way from first on Willie McCovey's single. Bob Will, the Cubs right fielder, charged in on the ball and threw a relay to Jerry Kindall, second sacker. When Mays rounded third the ball was still in flight, with Kindall out on the edge of the grass waiting for it.

Willie lit out around third without breaking stride. It was his own decision. "If Will had thrown home I would never have tried to score," Mays explained afterward. "But when I saw it was going to be a cutoff I gambled on Kindall hurrying his throw. If the throw had been accurate, the play would still have been close enough for me to knock the ball out of the catcher's hands."

As the play developed, Kindall threw into the dirt and the ball got away from Catcher Moe Thacker. The game was over.

When I was a guest in his home, Willie showed me his billiards room. He liked pool. "It's relaxing and sharpens my eyesight," he said. Willie was never a party thrower. "I just like to have a few friends over for a game of cards—four-handed whist, bridge, or gin rummy. Poker? I play a little. Stu Miller, Harvey Kuenn, Jim Davenport, and me like to play pinochle together."

Mays always kept a well-stocked wine locker with Scotch and bourbon, vodka and gin—the best brands. He never took a drink himself, but really enjoyed pouring for guests. Nor was he a book reader. "I'm a sports page and magazine man," he said. Novels didn't hold his interest. His library included a small *Webster's*, an encyclopedia, and a Bible.

When Billy Martin Came to Play

SPORTS FANS TODAY remember Billy Martin for his umpire bait-
ing and fiery fistics during a baseball field's off-hours. But there
was the active player side to his career, now all but forgotten,
and best illustrated by the final game of the 1953 World Series.

The Series was over and the incredible Yankees and even
more incredible Casey Stengel had won their fifth straight world
championship. And with the travail of Volga boatmen, the sullen Brooklyn Dodgers shuffled off the field, dragging their blud-
geons behind them, having, for the seventh time, failed to win
baseball's big 'un.

In a bleak atmosphere of cold wind and sullen skies, which
had forced umpires to turn on the lights, Yankee Billy Martin,
beyond dispute the hero of this Series, shot a grass-cutter single into center field in the ninth inning to score Hank Bauer
from second with the winning run.

Maybe Martin was just taking up where he had left off in the
1952 Fall Classic, when he had made the key catch of a wind-
blown pop fly that saved the Yankees' necks in the deciding
game of that one. But it is of the 1953 Series I now speak.

Martin never once stopped haunting the Dodgers in this one.
From the day he drove in the first three Yankees runs, with a
screaming triple in the first inning of the opening game, right
down to the end, when he broke up the series with his spectacular triple that broke the Dodgers' hearts and those of all

their passionate followers, the competitive spirit of the one-time urchin of the Oakland streets never flagged once.

While Mickey Mantle and Joe Collins were striking out eight times, Martin, who was thrilled by the packed stands and hub-bub and bedlam of a World Series, was hitting everybody, every day. In no one game or inning did he let down.

And Martin's name was on everybody's lips, even the pursed ones of those in the rival Dodgers clubhouse. Charlie Dressen, Dodgers manager, who would have gladly given his right arm to beat the damn Yankees, was higher in his praise than anybody.

"Why, the little stinker is the best player they've got," he was saying in the clubhouse moments after the Series ended. "He'll cut you, trip you—anything to beat you. And to think I helped teach him the game when he played for me out on the Coast just a couple of seasons ago. I feel like the man who has just been slapped in the face by his own son."

"Dressen didn't tell you the half of it," hoarsely yelled sixty-three-year-old Stengel who, unprecedentedly, had just won his fifth baseball championship. "Martin is the best second base-man in the world. That hit of his in the ninth gave me the biggest thrill I've gotten out of my forty years in baseball. I started him out as a raw kid in Oakland and he has made me a better man than I ever was."

But if Martin had to do with the making of Stengel, surely Ol' Case played a big role in the making of Martin, for Billy was just a throw-in player in the deal that sent Jackie Jensen up from the Coast League to the Yankees. The Yank front office balked at Billy, saying he was "too anemic" to make the grade in the majors. It was Stengel who insisted on Martin coming along with Jensen.

Billy's history-making single was his twelfth hit of the Series. Nobody ever made that many in six games. Sam Rice of the 1926 Washington Senators made twelve, but it took seven games.

It was a hitting series—17 homers (then an all-time Series record) and 120 base hits by the two clubs combined, with Martin showing the way with his 12 for an even .500 average, 2 homers, 2 triples, 5 runs scored, 8 more batted in, and 29 chances at second base without a bobble.

Billy's ninth inning single in this final game of the Series was almost anticlimatic, for a big thrill was the Dodgers top half of the ninth. With Brooklyn trailing 3-1, Carl Furillo, the National League's leading hitter of 1953, got a two-run homer to tie it up.

The mighty blow came off Allie Reynolds, who had come in to pitch in the eighth when Yankees starter Whitey Ford tired. Allie walked Duke Snider in this ninth after working the count to 3 and 2. He had the same count on Furillo, when the stocky outfielder got hold of an outside fastball and sent it towering into the tenth row of the right field stands, scoring Snider ahead.

The Yankees should never have been forced into their half to win this spine tingler. The situations were there for a more humiliating score, with a perfect setup for two big Yankees innings in the first and second. Atrocious baserunning and two double plays, however, held the Yankees to two runs in these two frames.

The Dodgers sent their big ace, Carl Erskine ("Oiskin," in Brooklynese), in this final game, but he was only a shadow of what he was in the third game when he fanned fourteen Yankees. Carl didn't have the smoke and he was wild. Collins was Carl's lone strikeout victim this gray afternoon, and he was touched for six hits in the four he worked before being relieved for a pinch hitter.

Ford started, and until the sixth it looked for all the world as if he was going to close out another World Series as he had in 1950 when, as a rookie, he had won the final game against the lowly Phils before being drafted into the army.

But on this day Whitey had to have help from Reynolds, who was credited with the victory (his seventh in Series play), tying the then existing mark compiled by Red Ruffing. Ford held the Dodgers in check until the sixth. Up till that time he had fanned the great Snider three times.

The Dodgers tally in the sixth would never have been scored but for a mental lapse by Ford. Jackie Robinson had doubled with one out and easily stole third when Ford seemed oblivious to the fact that he had a runner on second. Robinson scored on the next play, on Roy Campanella's grounder.

Ford had another close call in the seventh. After Whitey got two outs, Billy Cox singled and Bobby Morgan, a smallish Oklahoman pinch-hitting for Pitcher Bob Milliken, hit one out to right field that backed Hank Bauer to the railing. Hank had to stretch to spear the ball. Had it been driven five feet farther, it would have gone into the seats for a two-run homer, tying the score.

Manager Stengel concluded that Ford was tiring and brought in Reynolds in the eighth, with the heavy end of the Brooklyn batting order up. With two out, Robinson touched Allie for a hard single to left, but the big Creek Indian had the satisfaction of whiffing Campanella for the final out of the eighth.

That the game ever had to go into the final half of the ninth was due to Yankees miscues in the early innings. They got two runs in the first, but might have gotten six or seven. Gene Woodling started things off by getting a walk. Collins fanned for his eighth strikeout of the Series. Bauer singled sharply to left. Yogi Berra doubled to right, Woodling scoring easily from second.

Martin hit a hot one down to Junior Gilliam at second, which was charged as a questionable error. This loaded the bags with one out, but instead of hitting the ball in the air, Gil McDougald tapped into an infield double play, ending the inning.

The second frame loomed as a wrecker, too, when Phil Rizzuto and Ford opened with singles. Woodling's outfield fly scored Rizzuto. Collins singled infield and Bauer walked to load the bases. Berra then lifted a high fly to Snider in center field, but Ford on third forgot to tag up and started back for the bag belatedly; Collins, coming from second, almost collided with him. As a result of Ford's lapse, Gilliam handled Snider's throw and relayed it to the plate for an apple-pie double play.

The Dodgers won the consolation prize for Series hitting, getting more base hits than the Yanks and finishing with a team average of .301 to the Yankees' .279.

Top Umpire Baiter: The Lip

PERHAPS THE TOP umpire baiter during my forty-two years of sportswriting would have to be Leo Durocher. When he managed the old Brooklyn Dodgers, they called him the King of the Rhubarbers. He made it a turbulent life for most of the umpires and even stepped on the toes of one, getting away with it though Commissioner Happy Chandler once banned him from baseball for six months. The Lip never struck an umpire, but he had fistfights with Rowdy Richard Bartell, Zeke Bonura, and Mickey Owen that I know of. As a player, he was the gassiest of the St. Louis Cardinals Gas House Gang of the early 1930s.

When Pearl Harbor came, Leo was thirty-six. They classified him 4F because of a punctured eardrum. But there was nothing wrong with his mouth. The Lip could really shoot it off at umpires. Many arbiters kicked him out of a game early rather than bandy words with him. However, two fine umpires who were good friends of mine, Babe Pinelli (in the National League for twenty-one years as a Blind Tom) and Hall of Famer Jocko Conlan, told me more than once Durocher's bark was worse than his bite.

Once Leo asked Jocko if he thought anyone paid his way into the ballpark to see him umpire. "No," said Jocko coolly, "but if you don't shut up and go back to your dugout, anybody who might have paid to see you today is going to be disappointed."

Wade "Red" Killefer, manager of the old San Francisco Mission Reds of the Coast League, was the meanest umpire baiter

I ever ran across in the minors. Red, from Paw Paw, Michigan, had a nasty habit of spitting at Blind Toms. For this, Pacific Coast League prexy Harry Williams once suspended him for sixty days, a severe penalty.

But Killefer found a way to bait umpires more effectively. He chewed raw garlic for a stomach ailment. Every game he brought a little brown sack of it to the ballpark, keeping it handy in the dugout. When a disputable play arose and the decision went against Red, he'd arm himself with a fresh stick of garlic and charge on home plate.

Umpire George Magerkurth, later a big-league arbiter, was his particular target. George dreaded seeing Killefer charge at him. He'd turn his back in a futile attempt to avoid the fumes but the nimble Red would dart around and again confront him, face to face, blowing garlic at him. I don't recall Magerkurth ever reversing a decision, but it must have influenced him in thinking twice before making a ruling against the Missions.

The most combative modern-day manager in the majors has to be Billy Martin, but he has toned down to such an extent in more recent years that he's all but lost his kick-out title. Umpire nagging is perilously close to having become a lost art.

The late Tommy Heath, who succeeded Lefty O'Doul as manager of the old Coast League Seals, was a genial sort off the field, but he had a slick, artistic way of getting under an umpire's skin. During a Los Angeles heat wave, when the Seals were playing down there, Umpire Ford kicked out a Hollywood Stars player. "What'd he call you?" Heath, who had strolled up to the plate, asked Ford.

"What's it to you?" Ford shot back.

To which Tommy replied, "Oh, I just wanted to know so I can call you a so-and-so myself and get kicked out of this hot-box." Heath got what he wanted. Ford chased him.

Frank Lucchesi, former manager of the Phils and other big-league clubs, managed to lead every minor league he managed in the number of kick outs per season. Bobby Bragan, former president of the Texas League, as well as field manager in the minors and majors, was another holy terror with the umps.

Eddie Mulligan, a player-manager, was a very religious man known never to utter a profane word. But he could make umpires livid by dressing them down with such classic language as, "You yellow-livered meathead!" Thus, because he didn't actually curse, he usually escaped banishment.

Freddy Hutchinson, former Cincinnati and St. Louis manager, was a top umpire haranguer. He had a terrible temper. Managers often have to restrain their players during a rhubarb with the umpire, but players used to have to restrain Fred.

The old Portland club used to have some fine umpire-baiting managers. One was Bill "Raw Meat" Rogers, so called because every night he had a heavily salted raw steak for dinner, the blood running out of it. Spencer Abbott was another Portland manager. He could bait an umpire like he could bait a fishhook. Abbott dearly loved a fistfight but knew he couldn't hit an ump and get away with it. He was known, however, to lock the clubhouse door after a losing game and challenge any player on his club to an old-fashioned alley fight.

Casey Stengel was no slouch when it came to combativeness with umpires. Rogers Hornsby, former St. Louis Browns and Seattle Pacific Coast League manager, was a good one, too, as was the late Charlie Dressen. And of course there were others who do not come to mind immediately.

I can think of many gentle managers, though, who rarely if ever tried to bait an umpire. Among those who stand out prominently in my memory are Connie Mack, Walter Alston, Bob Lemon, Bill Virdon, Harry Hooper, Frank Shellenback, Clyde King, Red Schoendienst, Fred Haney, Jerry Coleman, Carl Zamloch, Bob Scheffing, Bucky Harris, Gil Hodges, Bob Kennedy, Jimmy Dykes, Wes Westrum, Jim Turner, Stan Hack, and Al Lopez.

One for Casey

"TAKE GOOD CARE of that typewriter it was always pretty good to me." This was the complete, unpunctuated text of a telegram Casey Stengel sent to me the night I bade adieu to daily sports columning after forty-two years of it in San Francisco. My mill had been good to Casey, but he had also been mighty good to it over the years. Long before he managed the Yankees, when grist for columns was scarce I'd phone him at the Leamington Hotel in Oakland when he managed the Coast League Oaks and he never let me hang up without a good yarn.

Truly, Ol' Case's career was part of my typewriter. Then they flew him East and gave him the Yankees job. In spite of cracks by Eastern writers about his poor piloting record in the majors (never in the first division) I contended that anyone who could win a pennant in the Triple A minors, as he had just done by jockeying around daily broken-down old pitchers, infielders, and outfielders, could win in the majors. Oakland is where he learned from sheer necessity how to platoon, which he did with the Yankees, causing Eastern writers' eyes to pop.

Casey's chances with the Yankees that first season were so slim that of two hundred writers polled in the spring, only six picked his club to win. But Casey did win, and he was to triumph for ten pennants and eight World Series championships as manager of the Pin Stripers.

For years I made it a habit of beginning my New Year's Day

column with a Stengel interview. Name a better way to start off the New Year. I'd either phone him at his Glendale home or go to the bank where he was vice president.

As for his qualifications to run a bank, Casey pointed out that he'd learned about gold studying to be a left-handed dentist in Kansas City, putting gold fillings in teeth.

Ol' Case inhabited baseball dugouts for fifty-five years. He came within one pennant of tying John McGraw's all-time winning record, made the Yankees a household name, and all but created the New York Mets with his bare hands. And he was more than just a manager. He was baseball's greatest one-man public relations staff, as the Yankees found out after firing him.

A captivating talker, he referred to the press as "you writin' fellers," and he'd give the reporter from the *Peoria Bugle* as much attention as a big New York syndicated writer, provided the question asked wasn't a silly one. His conversation meandered from cabbages to kings to Joe DiMaggio or Allie Reynolds. He'd often spin some irrelevant anecdote, completely out of context, about the time when he managed the Toledo Mudhens.

But he'd also talk good old meat-and-potatoes baseball, providing the most readable quotes you could ask for, all of which made sense. On other occasions, he'd ham it up in Stengelese when he'd speak English with all the clarity of a Peruvian yak. When he finished talking, you'd sort out your notes not quite sure of what you had—but it was always something entertaining. And your column read better if you didn't change a word. Once, explaining why he had just made the surprise move of leading off with Bob Cerv in a World Series opener, he said, "It was for the purpose of buntation." Tickled at having coined a new word, he added, "As for buntation Cerv can lay one down as good as Rizzuto."

Thinking back on all the World Series I covered (and they included all of Stengel's), and all the good copy that flowed from his glib, humorous tongue, I concluded that for all his clowning it up, he was truly the wise man of baseball of his day.

He'd come into the dugout two hours before game time and there was never a beginning or end to his discourses. You could be there at the start, just show up in the middle, or start out with him, take a coffee break, and come back to be in on the finish. He kept rambling on, but you could always piece together an entertaining column with apparent coherency and continuity, interspersed with anecdotes (like the day he tipped his cap to an umpire and a canary flew out of it).

And all the time he was sitting there holding court in the dugout he wasn't missing a trick on the field. He was often prescient. One World Series afternoon in the 1950s, just before game time for the opener, he suddenly scratched Gene Woodling from his batting order. A groin injury, Casey thought as he watched Woodling shag flies, was slowing him up half a step.

Woodling discovered his name crossed off in the batting order at Brooklyn's Ebbetts Field and was furious. He glared at Stengel as he passed him on the bench.

"Hoppin' mad, eh?" Casey said, delighted. "That's just the way I want him. Along about the seventh inning I just might use him for a pinch hitter and he just might (Casey pointed a finger to right field) rammycackle one against that Baker Beer sign out there."

This was exactly what Gene did—and in the seventh inning, too—hitting one against the screen for a triple that won the game.

In the 1959 World Series, the old Milwaukee Braves won three of the first four games; Brave Lew Burdette, a big blowhard West Virginia right-hander, popped off. Asked by a writer where the Yankees would finish if they were in the National League, Lew cracked, "Oh, about third or fourth."

After the Series ended and the Yanks had won out four games to three, Casey whispered to us with a wink, "You goin' over to that other clubhouse? Ask that feller if he still thinks we'd finish third or fourth in their league."

Stengel was no alibi artist. When Warren Spahn beat him in a World Series game, Yankees players complained to him that the umpires were calling balls as strikes. Casey didn't coddle them. "Look here, just a minute," he said. "You had a big round bat. He had a little round ball which got to look as small as a mothball to you hitters. You say he struck you out four times when they wasn't strikes, but it was an American League umpire calling 'em behind the plate."

When Burdette beat them three times in the 1957 World Series, Yankees players bellyached that he was throwing the spitter. "He did throw a peculiar pitch," said Casey, "but if a man can get away with it in a World Series with six umpires on the field, he's entitled to it and don't you come around whinin' to me. He was a good pitcher with the count three and two. He fidgeted around out there on the mound and talked a lot to his catcher and you guys let it irritate you."

I don't believe Casey really wanted to go back into baseball as Mets manager after the Yankees fired him. But he felt he owed it to George Weiss, and his pride was hurt when the Yankees didn't give him a chance to win another pennant and beat John McGraw as the winningest manager of all time.

Stengel never would have retired as Mets manager in the 1960s if he hadn't fractured a hip worse than he ever fractured the English language. That last year in command, the Mets didn't get into San Francisco by air until eight in the morning. Casey sat around the Jack Tarr Hotel lobby gabbing for two hours before going to his room. "I ain't taken a sleeping pill in my life," he said.

"When we invented the Mets," he mentioned, "the league let us buy twenty-two players from them. Only trouble is, we got those players late in life. We could only use their children or grandchildren. Our players have supplied Johns Hopkins and the Mayo Clinic with discoveries that have advanced the art of bone mending by one hundred years."

But the Mets outdrew the Yanks by half a million as soon as the newer New York club moved into Shea Stadium. Yet every club in the National League was making deals except his Mets, and this made Casey fume. "Don't the other clubs in our league appreciate the fact we have a terrific franchise?" he asked me in disgust. "We love our fans as much as we adore the Chase Manhattan Bank," he continued, managing a chuckle, "and doubtless for the same reason. We now have a fine stadium with escalators, but we gotta win for these people who have banners that say 'Go Mets, Go!'

"Our fans stood up and cheered for us all last season, but how long will their enthusiasm last if we only win forty games, like in 1962? It's a shame to spoil all that fun and enthusiasm, but the league ain't giving us a chance to improve our club. Every time we try to make a deal we get a brush-off.

"We have wealthy ownership. Mrs. Joan Payson gives millions to art, and she'll spend just as much to get a good ball club. Why did the other clubs let us in the league if they didn't want us to become competitive?"

When the Mets finally made it, it was too late for Ol' Case to enjoy the fruits of victory, though he was the foundation of it all.

Stengel was not just great copy—I loved and respected him like a father. There was never anyone like him in baseball, and there probably never will be.

The Legendary Satchel Paige

As WITH MANY legendary sports stars, there are so many stories about Leroy Robert "Satchel" Paige that it's hard to separate fairy-tale fiction from fact. But when greats like Bob Feller and Dizzy Dean rated him the "best all-around" pitcher they ever glimpsed, one has to listen. The most remarkable thing about Satch was that he lasted so long.

In his prime he pitched year-round, performing in the Negro Leagues until their season ended, then barnstorming all over creation daily until it was time to report for spring training the next season. One year in the 1940s he pitched in 153 games and hurled 14 no-hitters.

The last time I saw Satch was in 1964 when he came into my San Francisco sports department while under contract in Alaska. I asked him if the Anchorage club was in organized baseball. He replied with his usual good humor, "No, they is in disorganized baseball."

He was wearing a loud Hawaiian shirt, his face was furrowed, and his wire-thin, six-foot-four frame gave him the look of an aging gnome on stilts. But he retained his great dignity and confidence in his pitching. His midnight-colored hair had no streaks of gray as he told us, "I'se no worrier. They told me at Mayo's the only thing they can't cure is worryin'."

How old was he in 1964? That's a good question—probably fifty-nine and still pitching. Official baseball records list him as having been born July 7, 1906, in Mobile, where Willie Mc-

Covey and Hank Aaron had come from. This would have made him seventy-five when his heart gave out and he passed into the great beyond.

Satch never would tell his true age and got a little irked when people asked. He'd claim a goat ate the family Bible with his birthdate in it. He had recently attended his ma's funeral. She died in Alabama at age 104.

Whatever Satch's exact age, his baseball career was longer than anybody's. He broke in with the Chattanooga Black Lookouts in 1926, and ended his major league career with the old Kansas City Athletics in 1965 by pitching three scoreless frames in relief.

Much happened in those intervening years. "I waited the first twenty-two of 'em to get to the big leagues," he mentioned without a trace of rancor. He was forty-two when he finally made it.

In the 1930s Satch brought his Homestead Grays to the Coast and they played a group of major league all-stars around California. At old Seals Stadium, he pitched two shutouts in a row, beating first Bob Feller, then Diz Dean.

"They had Hack Wilson, Babe Herman, Charlie Gehringer, and the two Waner brothers—five .300 hitters, all following each other. In that first game I fans myself twenty-two." Satch was a little high on the number, but not by much. He did whiff sixteen. All this was fifteen years before he got to the majors.

Monte Irvin was with the Newark Eagles when Satch was in his prime. Irvin claimed, without a radar gun for proof, that Satch's ball crossed the plate with such speed it whistled—or made sort of a whirling noise, at any rate.

Not everybody agreed, among the dissenters being Wally Berger, Sloppy Thurston, Earl Averill, Smead Jolley, and the DiMaggio brothers. Larry French, ex-Pirates pitcher who barnstormed against Satch, thought he threw at about ninety-three miles per hour. "His ace in the hole was control," Larry told me recently in San Diego, where he is now a retired navy captain. "His competition in the Negro league wasn't as stiff as in the majors, but if he hadn't gotten to the bigs so late in life, he might be rated right up there with Johnson, Feller, Mathewson, Ford, Hubbell, and Koufax."

Satch was just one day shy of forty-two before he was allowed to pitch in the majors. Many think he should have had the honor of becoming the first black to come up, instead of the much younger Jackie Robinson. But Satch wasn't even the second choice. Larry Doby, Hank Thompson, and Willard Brown all beat him to the big tent.

There was no big rush to take on blacks in 1945, but by 1951, five big-league clubs were carrying them on their rosters and all finished in the first division.

In 1948, Owner Bill Veeck of the Cleveland Indians paid Satch forty thousand dollars—big money in those days. Even so, it cost Paige money. He was making more as a barnstormer. He earned his Cleveland salary the very first game he started, when more than fifty thousand watched him shut out the White Sox.

"They was thousands more outside waitin' to get in," he said while sitting by my desk. "They broke down the iron gate that must've weighed ten tons. They loved to see old Satch mow 'em down." And, he added with a chuckle, "I loved it, too."

At the next game, in Washington (never a big-draw city for baseball), seventy-three thousand watched. That season the Indians drew 2.5 million at home, ¼ million more than the Yankees. Yet many criticized Veeck for signing "an old man." They said it was just a box office gimmick, but Satch took him off the hook by pitching twenty-one games the rest of the season and finishing with a 6-1 won-and-lost record.

Cleveland won the pennant and Satch finally realized his dream of pitching in a World Series that fall, but only for two-thirds of an inning, in relief, allowing no hits or runs.

I asked Satch who were the toughest hitters for him to get out in major competition or along the barnstorming trail. "Ted Williams among lefty hitters and Joe DiMaggio against righties," he said without hesitation. "Yet I'd rather pitch to either than to Yogi Berra." Why? "Because he was the most deadly bad ball hitter I ever faced. He always murdered me."

Stories about Satch's pitching style are legion. Once, when with the Kansas City Monarchs, he called the outfield in and proceeded to strike out the side. His most famous delivery was called "the hesitation pitch." He used it in the black leagues, but major league umpires called this pitch a balk.

He had a pickoff to second base in which he threw the ball backhanded accurately to the bag on a signal from the catcher, not even bothering to look back. Nobody dared to take a big lead off the bag. It was great box office. The late Abe Saperstein should have signed him with the Harlem Globe Trotters.

During the many years when blacks were barred from organized ball, Satch's clubs would play about 130 Negro League games, then about 120 barnstorm exhibitioners—250 contests a year. Small wonder they called him "the Satchel," for he lived out of one. The players traveled by bus. Sometimes they'd play three games in twenty-four hours—one in the afternoon, one at twilight, followed by one at night forty miles farther along the route.

It was rough going. Often the blacks couldn't find a hotel that would take them in and had to sleep on the bus. In his later years as a major leaguer, Satch was allowed to use his own way of conditioning himself. Once when he was with the St. Louis Browns, the club played an exhibition game at Corpus Christi on the way home to open the season. Players took taxis to the ballpark from the train, but no cabdriver would take a black. So Satch went back to the train and slept through the night game. Manager Rogers Hornsby fined him one hundred dollars for not showing up, but Veeck, then president of the club, refused to dock him.

At the age of forty-six Satch was good enough to post a 12-10 record with the lowly Browns. He was inducted into the Hall of Fame at Cooperstown along with two Californians, Harry Hooper and Chick Hafey.

Baseball Has Changed

YOU SAY BASEBALL hasn't changed? There's a difference of night and day between spring training today and the camps of a generation ago. Veterans of the past will tell you it's like two different worlds. Probably the biggest change is equipment in the trainer's room. But the fabulous meal money allowance is another big item baseball vets also mention.

I asked Gene Mauch, managing the California Angels again, to name some of the changes. "Meal money," he began. "Kids today leave more tip money then we used to get to eat on."

The daily allowance is forty-two dollars, just for food. But if a player brings his family to camp, laundry and rent counts up to as much as five hundred dollars a week. Some players save enough off it to live free for several months.

Mauch broke in with the Brooklyn Dodgers in 1944, a war year when they trained at Bear Mountain, near New York City. "The biggest changes are in the trainer's room," he says. "Trainers today are more knowledgeable—they have an assistant to help and all sorts of fancy equipment.

"A big thing is that the whole concept of weights has changed. Back in 1944 the thinking was they made a player muscle-bound, but today they're big stuff."

Calisthenics? They were a joke. In Lefty O'Doul's day, they consisted of the squad starting the day's workout by lining up in center field and racing to home plate, where the manager had placed a ten-dollar gold piece that went to the winner.

Today, calisthenics are a must, often comprising long aerobics drills set to music.

Harry Dunlop of Sacramento, now the Padres bull pen coach, broke in with the Pirates when they trained in San Bernardino. He was an eighteen-year-old catcher, and rookies weren't too welcome in the batting cage. "It was three days before they let me swing a bat," he says.

The most significant thing Dunlop reports is that today's athletes come into camp better conditioned. "They report ready to play. After all, the main reason for spring training is to ready pitchers' arms. You rarely see a player report sporting a beer belly anymore."

Another change, Dunlop says, is the fewer number of sore arms. Trainers once got along with rubbing alcohol, Ben Gay, absorbine, Omega Oil, and rubbing the muscles. The hands are used very little today. Instead, the training room is full of gadgets—whirlpool tubs, bicycles, electric vibrators, and so on—that do the work of hand rubbing.

"Today you see a player sitting on the training table with a bag of ice taped to his elbow. This was unknown in my day," Dunlop says. "It came in with Sandy Koufax, I think, and it has even shoved Jacuzzis on the back burner. Ice not only heals a sore arm but prevents one from developing.

"There were plenty of sore arms in the old days, but you never heard about them. Unless you were a big star, you were scared to tell the trainer, because he'd tell the manager and you might be released."

Jerry Coleman, now the Padres' broadcaster, spent his first spring as a Yankee in Florida in 1947. He thinks a big change for the better about spring training is that there is now only one workout, a longer one, instead of the old two-a-day routine. "And the number of players in camp has been cut. We used to invite fifty and all of us didn't get enough work and instruction."

111

Coleman also points out that instead of counting the innings pitchers work in exhibitions, managers now have it figured down to the number of pitches, which they watch closely to prevent sore arms. After about fifty pitches in early spring games, you're out of there.

"Another thing, ball players have better parks to play in. In my day our Al Lang Field in Fort Lauderdale was Florida's only modern one," says Coleman. "The rest of them were rickety old wooden structures about ready to collapse.

"Players never had it as good as today. The big shoe companies give regulars their playing shoes free in return for an endorsement. The same goes for other equipment, except bats—players still have to buy them."

Billy Werle, former Seals and Pirates pitcher, now West Coast scout for the Orioles, spent a luxurious early spring training at Hana, Maui, when Paul Fagan had the club. His first big-league camp was in San Bernardino with the Pirates under easygoing Manager Billy Meyer.

"Nearly every athlete comes to camp today in great physical shape," Werle says. "They make big money now and can afford to work out in the winter. In my day I had to put in eight or ten hours a day in a warehouse or doing odd jobs. I didn't have time to work out on the side. We had to wait for spring training.

"The big change in spring training today is the trainer's room. Trainers know more about human anatomy and have more equipment to work with. Nowadays basketball, football, and baseball trainers get together and compare notes.

"There is more helpful surgery. In my time, few of us would submit to an operation, for fear one would wreck our career. Surgeons were outsiders. Today they are specialists who have made a study of baseball arms and bones. Look at what happened to Tommy John. They just about transplanted a whole arm and made a new pitcher out of him."

Jack McKeon, the Padres' general manager, never got to the majors as a player. He was a catcher in the Pirates chain and later managed in the minor and major leagues, including with the Oakland Athletics.

"Training camp expenses have become fabulous," says McKeon. In his day, players either ate at a training table or got $3.50 a day for meals and felt like it was stealing. Coffee was a nickel and a hamburger fifteen cents.

McKeon notes there are very few country boys coming to camp fresh off the farm anymore—kids who've never been away from home before. It robs camps of much humor and atmosphere.

"Personnel has undergone a great change. A few years ago, a collegiate man in baseball was singled out as an oddity. Today, two-thirds of baseball's major leaguers either graduated from college or had a couple of years of it.

"Kids today aren't hell-raisers. I mean guys that go out on the town during spring training. They're serious young fellows who come to camp self-disciplined. They aren't the carousing type. They come bent on making the club, not on having a good time with night life."

The changes in baseball equipment do not end in the trainer's room. A first baseman's glove is long, with a deep pocket so the player can reach bad throws and scoop low ones out of the dirt.

The *Sporting News'* Spink, Editor of the Baseball Bible

NOW THERE WAS a newspaperman for you—J. G. Taylor Spink, owner and editor of the *Sporting News* of St. Louis from 1914 (when he succeeded his father) until 1962, when he died from emphysema at the age of seventy-four. The *Sporting News* was (and still is) known as the Baseball Bible, though today it dabbles in all sports. For years Spink's publication handled the MVP awards, until he turned the chores over to the Baseball Writers' Association of America. Spink also inaugurated such awards as the annual rookie, outstanding pitcher, and relief pitcher awards.

Taylor, as nearly all of us called him (or to some, Mr. Spink), was something straight out of *The Front Page*, the Broadway stage hit of long ago. The old cliché "They threw away the mold when they made him" certainly applied to this rare sports personality. As a newspaperman he was tops. He could smell a story before it happened and was relentless in pursuit of facts. His workweek was a straight seven days; his days a straight twenty-four hours. He worked around the clock and expected the correspondents he hired to do the same.

I was his San Francisco man for twenty-six turbulent but exciting years. News excited him and he communicated that excitement to his writers, who in turn couldn't help but convey it to readers. Nobody ever put Alexander Graham Bell's invention to more frequent and effective use. If he wanted to

114

reach you, he'd find you by phone. It was useless to try and hide—there was no place to run. What a pistol!

In all the time I wrote the Giants, 49ers, Coast League baseball, and assorted sports for him, one little incident stands out above the others. The phone range in my San Francisco home. My wife answered. "Who is calling?" she asked.

"J. G. Taylor Spink of the *Sporting News*," came the cocky, petulant reply.

"What time is it in St. Louis, Mr. Spink?" my wife asked softly.

"Eight o'clock," was the impatient answer.

"Well, Mr. Spink, it may be eight o'clock there, but it's only six here and still dark. I'm not going to wake my husband up at this ungodly hour for you or anybody else after he had a hard night at the office."

"But this is *important*," said the gravel-gruff voice on the other end.

"I don't care how important it is," my wife replied. "Call back at a decent hour." With that, she hung up. Taylor must have been fuming at the other end. How many people talked up to him like that and got away with it?

Important? Every hour in his day and everything he did was important. He moved from one "crisis" to another. I was amazed when my wife repeated the conversation a few hours later. Shortly afterward he phoned, humbly apologizing to my wife first.

That was J. G. T. S. He was a man of contrasts and contradictions. He could be kind, generous, and gentle, or intolerant, stingy, and unforgiving.

Once he wanted a three thousand five hundred-word article from Ty Cobb for a book on how to steal bases. What better person to tell it than the Georgia Peach? I explained Ty was up in his summer home, just over the California border in Nevada.

"He has a phone, hasn't he?" Taylor asked sarcastically.

I explained, "I can't get a yarn like that from him over the phone. I'll have to sit down with him a couple of hours and I won't be able to get up there and do it till Saturday."

"Saturday?" fumed Taylor. "This is only Wednesday!" He almost threw a fit. Everything with him and the *Sporting News* had to be "right now." But I told him my first duty was to my own paper. I got the long piece he wanted, however, and was handsomely rewarded with one of those yellow *Sporting News* checks.

He kept a constant feel on what was going on in baseball. Often he knew more about what was cooking than the man on the beat. Once he phoned (this was in the days before the Giants came West) wanting a thousand words "right now" (as always) on Clarence "Pants" Rowland.

"An obit?" I asked innocently. "When'd he die?"

"Obit, hell," Taylor hissed. "The man isn't dead. He's going to be elected president of the Coast League in forty-eight hours and I've just got time to catch the edition." It was all news to me, close to the picture, and supposedly right on top of things. But Taylor had the scoop.

There was the time he called and asked if I'd ever written a book. At the time I hadn't and told him so. "Well, you're going to right now—half a book. Ty Cobb has cancer and the docs give him only six weeks to live. You and Harry Salsinger (Detroit sports editor) are going to write a book called *The Cobb I Knew*. I want the copy in a week. I know you're a fast writer and can get it to me that soon."

I was to write of Ty's boyhood and the stormy years after he left baseball, and Salsinger was to take care of his playing career. I took a week off from the paper and drove myself hard to write nearly 250 pages. The deathless prose never did see the light of day because Salsinger got sick and didn't half finish his job. By the time he did, Cobb had died and the book market was flooded with biographies on him.

But was Taylor cheap? Don't you believe it! I received a check that astounded me.

Taylor groomed his son, C. C. Johnson Spink, to succeed him. He advised him, "Johnson, you'll find it necessary to work long hours until you're forty years old."

"What happens after I'm forty?" asked the son.

"By that time you'll be used to it."

Johnson followed the advice about long hours and after a few years went to his doctor for a checkup. The physician advised him to rest and relax at least two days a week.

Taylor was incredulous. "The SOB is a quack," he shouted at Johnson. "He oughta be investigated by the medical society."

In spite of his gruff exterior and insistent demands on his writers, Taylor was a delightful man when relaxed. If you caught him away from the office, he was a different person. I'm recalling now the time I was in St. Louis for a crucial Giants-Cardinals series. Taylor invited Bob Stevens of the *San Francisco Chronicle* and me to his house that Saturday night. We had cocktails and dinner in his lovely home and there couldn't have been more congenial hosts than Taylor and his charming wife, Blanche.

After dinner he drove us to one of the city parks for a big public fireworks display. He was like a little boy in his enchantment over the exploding skyrockets and pinwheels.

Fagan's Ban
on Ballpark Peanuts

PAUL FAGAN, one-time owner of the San Francisco Seals, envisioned major league baseball coming to the Coast a good ten years before the slower-thinking, Eastern moguls tumbled to the idea. If they had accepted Fagan and his plan, there would have been no Candlestick Park. For Paul, who had a penchant for surveys, had already decided to make Seals Stadium, close to downtown, a double-decker and to build an elaborate underground parking system.

Few were privy to seeing the architect's blueprints for this layout, but Paul showed them to Joe Orengo and me one day, and they were fantastic. As things have turned out, the National League would have been wise to accept Fagan and his Seals Stadium plan.

Baseball in the old Coast League had its characters and laughs, more so than the modern big-league game. It was Fagan's weakness for having surveys made that created one of the most amusing incidents I have ever come across in sports.

One day while calling Brick Laws, owner of the Oakland Oaks, I kept getting a busy signal. When the line finally cleared, I kidded Laws, asking if he were closing a big deal with the Yankees for the sale of his big star, Artie Wilson, the base stealer.

"No," Brick informed me, "I was talking to Fagan. He's outlawing the sale of peanuts at the park because they cost too much to sweep up."

I phoned Fagan and our conversation resulted in what was

called "the Great Peanut Episode," every bit as gripping as the Great Train Robbery of 1896!

Yes, it was true, Fagan admitted. There would be no peanuts sold at Seals Stadium when the season opened in a few weeks.

It sounded incredible. We were close friends, and even at the risk of spoiling a dandy yarn, I tried to talk him out of it. I told him ballpark peanuts were a tradition, an institution, part of the game, reminding him of the baseball ballad, "Take Me Out to the Ball Game," the key line of which is, "Buy me some peanuts and Cracker Jack, I don't care if I never get back." I told him he'd be a laughingstock if he outlawed the peanut.

"Cracker Jacks are all right," Fagan replied. "We'll sell them, and popcorn too. But the peanuts must go. It isn't that I think eating peanuts is vulgar. I'm fond of them myself. But I've had a survey made, and it costs me thirty thousand dollars a season just to sweep up the shells. I lose five cents on every ten-cent bag of peanuts we sell."

He called peanuts "a nuisance," saying, "my janitors get them swept in a pile, then the wind comes along and scatters them all over the place again. You have to pick them up by hand, and using a vacuum sweeper won't do the job. Have you ever thought of how hard it is to get at a peanut shell in a corner? Those giant aisle brooms with their three-foot wingspread are no good for peanuts. You have to get down on your hands and knees with a whisk broom."

Fagan then explained that when he ate peanuts, he broke the shell in only two pieces. "But most fans crumple it up into a hundred tiny particles, not to play tricks on the management, but perhaps it's plain nervousness. Anyway, the wind scatters the pieces into nooks and crannies, making them almost impossible to get at. Popcorn and Cracker Jacks present no janitorial problems. If a few kernels fall on the floor, they don't stick."

Paul's decision was final, so I wrote the story. It made about every sports page in the country—in fact, it was the subject of comment on editorial pages from California to Maine.

About seventy-two hours later I scored another beat. Fagan phones to say he had rescinded the order banning peanuts at Seals Stadium. Proving himself a big man, he admitted it had been a blunder to give the peanut the heave-ho.

"I had no idea the thing would create such a furor," he said, "Why, even my gardener told me I was all wet, and my broker phoned from New York asking why I did such a fool thing. I've read the papers and listened to all the newscasts, and now I know I made a big mistake."

He added, "The public's reaction was a gold mine to me. Many corporations spend thousands, even millions on surveys to find out what the public wants. I've found people want peanuts with their baseball. They shall have them, with the shells on."

Another thing had influenced him. "Thousands of peanut pickers in Virginia, North Carolina, and Georgia would be out of work if all ballparks banned the goober. I've had wires from both growers and pickers, and both are on my neck."

But he still staunchly defended the economics of his peanut ban. "It costs me plenty to sweep up the shells, but hang the expense. The fans come first."

So not only was the lowly peanut back at Seals Stadium forever, but Fagan also ordered a large bag to be presented free of charge to each fan passing the turnstiles opening day. As it turned out, 18,400 fans were there—a banner crowd. At 50 peanuts to the bag, 900,000 free ones were passed out—with the result that about 20 billion shell fragments had to be swept up. Free peanuts on the house had cost Fagan over four thousand dollars—plus the sweep-up bill.

Even as he was putting the peanut back on its pristine pedestal, his field manager, Frank O'Doul, was promising further use of the goober by saying, "If we do not finish in the first division, I'll roll a peanut with my nose all the way to Market Street from the Ferry Building to Twin Peaks." And the luncheon group he told this to held him to his promise.

Searching for the All-Time, All-Around Athlete

WHO WAS THE greatest all-around athlete of all time? Athletes' marks keep on improving the record books in nearly all sports, but I'm not writing here about those in one sport. I'm talking about the old-fashioned, all-around performer.

If you watched "Superstars"—a TV series in which you saw such so-called supers as Reggie Jackson, Mike Schmidt, Steve Garvey, et al., compete in a Christmas mix of different sports—you must have been impressed with the fact that the modern "super" guys can't compete with the likes of Jackie Robinson, Jim Thorpe, Enrie Nevers, Bob Mathias, Jesse Owens, and others as mythical great all-around athletes.

Athletes who excel in more than one (sometimes as many as four or five) different sports are as rare as no-hit pitching performances, but I'm not sure after naming the above standouts I included the number one all-arounder.

Some might claim that Pheidippides could have won the all-around title hands down if he had been around today. Running twenty-two miles with his dying breath to inform Athens of the great Greek victory over the Persians in the Battle of Marathon in 490 B.C. was one of his big feats. He was not only a great runner, but could also have garnered gold medals in many sports.

I'm withholding the name of a real sleeper—a genuine dark horse—until later in this chapter. The name is sure to surprise you. But for now, the guy who gets my vote as the super of supers is Jackie Roosevelt Robinson. He surely was a stand-out all-arounder.

Robinson was the first black ever to play in the majors. He was a stick-out fielder, hitter, and base stealer; led the National League three or four different seasons in stolen bases; and I saw him join the handful of players who stole home in a World Series during a Yankees-Dodgers Fall Classic in old Ebbetts Field, Brooklyn. He also posted the top fielding average for National League second basemen for several seasons, and either broke or equaled a number of all-time marks to become an MVP and a resident of Cooperstown.

But this isn't the half of it. He was also an all–Pacific Coast Conference basketball scoring champion, and not just a good, but a great, halfback for UCLA, with a long list of great open-field runs. In 1939, he averaged twelve yards per carry (a UCLA record), and in 1940 he averaged twenty-one yards per punt return. The story goes he broke eighty the first time he wielded a golf club. He also won tennis tournaments. And he was an excellent bridge player. Guess he could do anything but cook.

Mathias's winning of the 1948 Olympic gold medal in London as a seventeen-year-old stamps him as an outstanding all-arounder—and a natural one, for he had never even competed in some of the decathlon events when he won, but had studied the techniques in a paperback instruction book. He proved it was no fluke when he again won the decathlon event four years later with a record at Helsinki.

The kid from Tulare had a brilliant if brief career in football at Stanford. He didn't choose to play the game during his entire college career, but his ninety-four-yard return of a second-half kickoff in the Los Angeles Coliseum against the heavily favored Trojans to produce an upset win is a revered legend in Palo Alto. Had Mathias chosen to turn pro instead of run for Congress he might have made fans forget Cleveland's Jim Brown, the peerless running back. And had he turned his talents to baseball, it is said he could have been a home-run hitter in a class with Ralph Kiner, Lou Gehrig, Roger Maris, Hack Wilson, Hank Greenberg, et al.

Ernie Nevers belongs high on any list of great all-arounders. He always fluctuated with Thorpe between number one and number two on Pop Warner's list of the greatest fullbacks he had coached; as a pro, Nevers scored every point of the forty in a Cardinals smasher win over George Halas's Chicago Bears.

Ernie might have been a great pitcher but for an arm injury incurred in football. Even so, he pitched in the majors. Two of Babe Ruth's homers the year the Bambino hit sixty were off him. Nevers pitched for the St. Louis Browns until Manager Dan Howley caught him diagraming football plays in mid-July while sitting in the Browns' dugout during a game. That did it. Howley sent him down the river to the Mission Reds of the Coast League.

Which brings me to Thorpe. The Carlisle Indian, a great decathlon man, won the event in the Olympics and was the record holder until Mathias came along. Once Thorpe recorded eight firsts in a dual track meet against Lafayette College. He could do everything but pole vault, and they say he could have won a gold medal in every other Olympics event but crocheting and basket weaving.

His football feats against Harvard while at Carlisle are well known, as are those of his days at pioneering pro football, when he was still a tough man to tackle after passing at the age of forty. He was also a fine baseballer and might have been a ten-year man in the majors if his manager, John McGraw, hadn't disliked him and kept him with New Haven—the Giants' minor league farm club—beyond his time.

There have been other good all-arounders. One was Jackie Jensen. Sam Chapman of Cal and Connie Mack's Athletics is another. Lou Gehrig surely qualifies, as do Paul Giel of Minnesota, Wes Schulmerich, and Oscar Eckhardt, owner of the highest batting average in the eighty-one-year history of the Coast League.

Which brings me to the sleeper mentioned earlier. He has been badly overlooked in my rundown. He's Jesse Hill, who wound up as USC athletic director. He was an intercollegiate long jump champion in track and field, and was also in the majors, playing for none other than the Yankees and setting a high standard for outfielders. And as a fullback on one of Howard Jones's finest teams—1929—he led the conference in yardage gained per carry (8.2). Hill isn't as well known as some other old-time USC stars like Frank Gifford, Orv Mohler, Ernie Pinckert, Mort "Devil May" Kaer, Cotton Warburton, and the noblest Trojan of them all, Morley Drury. He just might have been, but Dean Cromwell, USC track coach, kept him from competing on the grid.

Cromwell finally relented and let Jesse compete, but not until he was a junior, when Jim Musick was entrenched at fullback—and Musick liked to play all sixty minutes. Hill wondered if he'd ever earn his letter. Finally, Musick was hurt early in a game against Washington in Seattle. In came an eager sub. In such a star-spangled group of Thundering Herdsmen as Garrett Arbelbide, Mohler, and others, Hill was just a number.

The sub ripped off a seventy-yard touchdown run the first time he packed the ball. Radiocasters reached for their lineup sheets to see who this number 32 phenom was. "Folks," the radio blared, "this fellow Cliff Thiedes is really something." Number 32 continued to tear up and down the field. "No question," rasped one veteran announcer, "man and boy, I've glimpsed some great running backs in my day, but none could ramble like this Thiedes is doing today."

Seattle fans who had seen greats like Wilson and Tesreau agreed no one was number 32's equal. "Where," asked the announcer, "has the coach been hiding this boy?"

Thanks to number 32, almost a one-man team, USC won.

The most surprised person among the radio listeners in Los Angeles was Thiedes himself. Coach Jones had left him at home "because he wasn't quite good enough to make the traveling squad." The guy who was so spectacular was none other than Jesse Hill, who had put on the number 32 jersey by mistake.

Memorable Sports "Left Outs"

SPORTS ANNALS ARE replete with "left outs"—underrecognized and underplayed athletes. One could make them the theme for a book, but there's space here to delineate only a few. Among the "forgotten men" who never received proper recognition for their skills is the Bay Area's Dominic DiMaggio.

Only in Boston, where he played for years as a Red Sox outfielder, is Dom's great ability fully appreciated. The little brother of Joe lived in the Yankee Clipper's shadow all his baseball life, though he was one of the better hitters for average and a top defensive man throughout his career.

He was deceiving as a ball player due to his diminutive size and to the fact that he wore glasses. When he reported to the Seals for a tryout, a frail, delicate-looking boy of nineteen, he was wearing a Galileo High sweater and big, dark-rimmed specs. Charlie Graham, president of the Seals, was accused of just trying to make a fast buck off of Joe's fame when the club signed Dom.

Even Lefty O'Doul, who was later to manage him into the majors, scoffed at the thought of the bespectacled Dom ever amounting to much of an athlete. Johnny Gill was to be the Seal's right fielder that spring. A giant of a man who swung a big bat, he had just come down from the Cubs. Curious as to who would play alongside of him in center, Gill asked, and when they pointed to Dom, he was aghast. "That little squirt?" Gill asked in disbelief.

But he soon changed his tune. "You take it, Dom," Gill would yell, because Dom not only played center but also caught many of the flies in Gill's area as well.

Joe DiMaggio just missed leading the American League in RBIs for 1941 and after the season ended, Joe told me why he didn't make it.

"During a Red Sox series in Yankee Stadium, I hit a line drive to left center with the bags bulging," Joe explained. "It should have gone for a base hit and scored at least two runs, but Dom played me too short and made a shoestring catch. That night we went to dinner and I told him, 'Dom, you're playing me too shallow in center. This isn't the Coast League you know. There are guys up here who hit the ball a country mile.'

"So the next afternoon there are two on and I got a hold of a pitch. I hit it nearly four hundred feet and who's standing there right underneath the flagpole but my brother. Those two 'hits' alone robbed me of the RBI title."

Another one of the undersung could-have-beens was Bo Belinsky, falsely pictured as an incorrigible playboy and robbed of a full pitching career that had been highlighted (as far as it went) by a no-hitter. I was in Palm Springs the day Bo first reported to Bill Rigney and the Angels. Belinsky was a southpaw, richly endowed with self-esteem. Writers said his key pitch, a screwball, best described his character.

His wisecracks caused some to peg him as an oddball. But by June he was 7-1 and had pitched a no-hitter. He was offered a role in a movie to be entitled, *The Walter Johnson Story*. But Rocky Bridges said, "You're a lefty. How can you play Johnson?" Bo cracked, "Let 'em reverse the negatives."

He sold the baseball he threw to complete his no-hitter for four thousand dollars and watched a video rerun of his performance. Asked what he thought of it, he wisecracked, "I need a haircut." The fan image of Bo was that he lived it up to the hilt from dusk to dawn, a tippler, womanizer and rowdy-dow.

"One drink was his limit," Rigney swears to this day. "He stayed in shape far better than many stars. He just had the bad habit of saying the first thing that came to his mind."

Bo should have lasted a lot longer than he did in the bigs because he could pitch. But he wound up in the minors.

Though he never received recognition for it, Art Nehf, one of the great pitchers in Giants history, played a part in the move of the majors to the Coast, in that he was the first base-baller to report for spring training by air. This was way back in 1929 when he flew a single-motor job from Phoenix, stopping at Brawley for gas and landing four hours later in Los Angeles at the Giants camp.

Mark Kelly, the Los Angeles sports editor, had been hammering away for major league ball in the Coast even that far back. He seized on this first flight by a ball player to training camp as proof positive that flying was practical for ball clubs.

"Kelly rounded up a huge crowd at the airport and I felt something like Lindbergh when he climbed out of his *Spirit of St. Louis* in Paris," Art once told me. "The papers spread photos all over page 1 of it and it really started the ball rolling in earnest for what finally resulted in the Dodgers and Giants coming West."

The Professional Golfers Association of America (PGA) circuit still regards George Bayer as capable of driving a golf ball farther than any mortal in the game, but the Bay Area once had a longer whacker in George Coffee ("Big George").

In the early 1930s, using a wooden hickory-shafter driver of 1920 vintage, Coffee outdrove opponents by 20 yards and more. No golfer was his equal for distance. Coffee could get on the green in one at the seventh hole at San Francisco's Harding Park—a drive of some 340 yards. A drive of 300 is regarded as phenomenal there because the air is heavy and wet grass diminishes the roll.

Coffee was destined for stardom. He was a full-fledged pro at the age of seventeen. But an injury resulted in the loss of a kidney, and this cost him a brilliant career on the national circuit.

There are "left outs" even among horses. You never hear Nashua's name mentioned in the same breath as such super equines as Man O'War, Citation, Equipoise, Seabiscuit, Pharlap, or Secretariat. But he could have been a Triple Crown winner if his trainer, Sunny Jim Fitzsimmons, hadn't erred.

The legendary Sunny Jim, who had saddled Omaha and Gallant Fox as Triple Crowners, told of his mistake months later. Swaps had beaten Nashua in the 1953 Kentucky Derby. "If I had known more about your California colt, I'd have raced Nashua differently against him in the Derby," Jim confessed. "I thought I had only Summer Tan to beat to win the Derby so I told Eddie Arcaro not to go chasing any other horse. Eddie followed my orders.

"As a result Nashua ran the first part of the race too slowly, but though he was closing much ground on Swaps in the stretch, he made his move too late."

Nashua easily outran Summer Tan and went on to win the Preakness and Belmont.

Taking the Mike for
Jack Dempsey

PERHAPS ONE OF the most bizarre (and surely the most unusual) experience I had in forty-two years of sportswriting was when I was "Jack Dempsey" on a radio show. This was certainly not by choice, however. Just a few weeks before this incident, the Manassa Mauler, always popular in San Francisco, had lost in a tragic effort to regain his title when he was given the famous "long count" in Soldier Field, Chicago (September, 1927), losing again to Gene Tunney.

Jack came to San Francisco to be consoled by old friends. My newspaper, the *Call Bulletin*, also owned at that time radio station KFRC in the Don Lee Cadillac Building on Van Ness Avenue, and when Pat Frayne, our boss and sports editor, invited Dempsey to be on our half-hour Friday night sports program, he readily accepted. He was stopping at the old Palace Hotel and told Pat not to bother sending a limo to get him—he knew where the station was and would hop a taxi.

When it neared 7:30 P.M., time for Pat, as emcee, to go on with the great ex-heavyweight champion, Jack was a no-show. Frayne had written a two-column box spread in all editions of the paper that day, announcing Dempsey as the big attraction. And Pat wasn't one to be easily put off.

About thirty seconds before the show began, Frayne told me, "He isn't coming. You're going to be Dempsey."

I was petrified. "What's he sound like?" I stammered.

"What're you gonna ask me and what am I going to use for an answer?"

"Shh!" whispered Frayne. "We're about to go on the air."

Seconds later a red light flashed over the big black box they used for a microphone in those days. Pat opened the show with, "Good evening, sports fans. We have a great treat for you tonight. Meet him—the one and only Jack Dempsey!"

"Hello, folks," I replied, throwing my voice into as deep a bass as I could. I figured a heavyweight champion had to have a deep voice; never having heard Dempsey on the air, I didn't know his voice was a falsetto, almost as high-pitched as a woman's. He was notorious for this.

Frayne continued, "How did it feel that hot July afternoon in Toledo when you knocked out Jess Willard to become heavyweight champion of the world? What punch did you use to score the kayo?"

Why I ever consented to go on as Dempsey I'll never know. The show was on now and I had to go through with it. "Well," I explained, still keeping my voice gruff, "it was sort of a combination left hook and right cross—a one-two punch, sort of." Actually, it had been a series of uppercuts.

Frayne then asked me, "How did you come to get knocked through the ropes and into the laps of ringside sportswriters the night you fought Angel Firpo?"

Answering this one I managed to gulp, "I just forgot to duck on of his roundhouse right-hand punches."

There followed another question or two, then Frayne gently put his hand on my shoulder and shoved me to one side. I looked up, startled, and there was Dempsey standing big as you please. His cab had been caught in traffic.

Pat continued plying the real Dempsey with questions, to which he always had interesting answers. Give him credit, he didn't blame Referee Dave Barry for giving Tunney the long count. Jack explained that he had failed to listen when Barry told them both in the center of the ring, just before the bell rang for the first round, that new Marquis of Queensberry rules required a boxer to go to a neutral corner immediately after flooring an opponent. This Dempsey failed to do.

Our radio show audience was left wondering why Dempsey's voice changed from a basso profundo to an almost tenor pitch in a matter of seconds, for Frayne never did explain there were two Jacks—myself and the real Manassa Mauler.

On one of his visits to San Francisco, I asked Dempsey who hit him the hardest, expecting that surely he would say Luis Firpo, "the Wild Bull of the Pampas." But no, Gunboat Smith packed the biggest wallop. Jack went a bit into detail. "In our first fight out at Recreation Park, I got hit with the most lethal punch I ever took from anybody. In fact, every time I come back here I feel my jaw to make sure it's still there."

Jack thinks that night with the Gunboat was the turning point in his career. He had knocked out the tough Charlie Miller in Oakland a month before and Jack "the Dapper Doc" Kearns, his manager, began talking big-money fights for him. "I can't tell you much about my fight with old Gunboat or the punch he landed, except from hearsay.

"All I remember, actually, is looking good in the first round of our four-rounder. The rest is pretty much of a blank. I knew he had a good right-hand punch and he knew I was open for it. So I guess it had to happen.

"Early in the second round, he belted me one on the chin. I have no recollection whatsoever of what happened after that."

The first thing Jack remembers was waking up in his room at the old Continental Hotel on Turk Street the next morning with a jaw he could hardly open. In the opposite twin bed was his (then new) manager, Kearns. "He shook me awake and I began to apologize for getting knocked out. I asked him what round Gunboat put me away in.

" 'Knocked out, hell,' Kearns told me. 'You won a sensational unanimous decision and it might get you a shot at champion Jess Willard. I'm going to work on it right now. You're ready to challenge him.'

"I still didn't believe Kearns, so I dressed quickly and went down to the lobby and bought a morning *Examiner*. There it was in studhorse-size type—a head three inches high, reading 'Dempsey Wins Big.' I must have stayed in the ring on instinct because to this day I can't remember a thing after Gunboat landed that one on my jaw."

The late Toby Irwin who refereed the fight told me a few years later that the whole ring shook, vibrated, and swayed with the impact of the blow and Dempsey hitting the canvas. "It was like a quake," said Irwin. "I thought the whole ring was going to collapse."

Dempsey told me Firpo's punch wasn't half as hard. "After he knocked me through the ropes and the round ended, I was sitting in my corner and Kearns was searching frantically in his pockets for the smelling salts. 'Where'd I put the bottle?' he asked me over and over. My head was clear. 'It is right in your pants pocket,' I told him. 'I saw you put it there when we left the dressing room.' My head was clearer than the Doc's."

Dempsey fought Willie Meehan twice in San Francisco before becoming champion. The initial bout is listed as a loss in Dempsey's record—the only defeat he'd had until he lost to Gene Tunney. But Meehan won by a ruse. It was to have been a no-decision four-rounder—really an exhibition.

"I floored him twice and when he got up he whispered, 'You're not going to make me look like a bum in my own hometown, are you, Jack?' The remark amused me, so I took it easy the rest of the way since it was only an exhibition. But at the finish Meehan rushed over and raised Referee Eddie Graney's hand and the crowd thought it was Graney doing it."

The record books recorded it erroneously as a win by Meehan. Dempsey later beat him easily.

For years Hollywood tried to film the story of Dempsey's life. It would have been a four-star winner as far as the plot goes. Both Dempsey and Tunney agreed to the film, but Kearns held out for too high a figure for his share of the rights. And no movie of the Manassa Mauler would have been complete without Kearns in it.

Such a film could have packed as much drama as *Pride of the Yankees*, the life story of Lou Gehrig. Dempsey would be the story—his poverty in the early days, his saloon fights, his trial for being a World War I slacker (he was acquitted), his marriage to Estelle Taylor (the movie queen), his wrangle with Kearns, and his bad luck in losing to Tunney in a fight he would have won but for the long count.

Those First-Round Kayos

FIRST-ROUND KNOCKOUTS—they're rare things indeed. One is my grand total. In the course of more than forty years in sports, covering fights off and on, the only one I ever actually witnessed was Young Corbett III of Fresno vs. Jimmy McLarnin, for the world welterweight title.

There are many different explanations for these one-round quickies. The victims often pass them off just by saying "I forgot to duck." Some call them the result of a "lucky punch" (and, chances are, it was). But in the case of Corbett-McLarnin, it was no fluke. McLarnin, "the Baby-Faced Assassin," could punch as if he had a stick of dynamite in each glove.

Some one-rounders are the result of trickery. A famous one in this category was when Kid McCoy, who fought in California, won the middleweight title from George Chip in Brooklyn. "Your shoelace is untied," McCoy said, and when poor George glanced down for a split-second, off-guard moment, McCoy clipped him on the chin.

Perhaps the most famous one-round kayo was by Joe Louis. Even casual boxing fans may recall it. In his second fight with Max Schmeling, the Brown Bomber tore into the German with savage fury from the start, not waiting to measure his opponent. He put him to sleep in two minutes, four seconds. Schmeling wasn't a bad guy. I interviewed him in Florida after the war while covering Patterson-Johansson in their third battle.

Probably no fighter in history—and make no mistake, Max

was a good one—was more decisively beaten in such a hurry. Joe first decked him for a three-count then came in with a left hook, followed by a right cross that sent his man to the canvas face down. Schmeling's handlers tossed in the towel and Ref Arthur Donovan awarded Louis a kayo win.

Some experts say a good fighter is never kayoed in the first round, but don't you believe it. It has happened to greats, near-greats, and ingrates, as they say. Al Hostak kayoed Seattle's Freddie Steele in one round, and Tony Canzoneri needed only two minutes, five seconds to finish Al Singer.

In California boxing history Corbett vs. McLarnin is the most memorable one-rounder. The Bay Area never had a more popular ring idol than Corbett, whose real name was Ralph Giordano. He was great box office. San Francisco had a very loyal Italian colony that doted on the rising youth pugilist. He could fight, too. His record was 136 wins and only 10 losses. Doubtless he would have made short shrift of guys like today's Sugar Ray Leonard or Roberto Duran.

Corbett, in his prime, couldn't walk down Market Street without being mobbed by adoring youngsters. Mothers wanted their sons to grow up and be "just like him." He beat such good ones as young Jack Thompson, Sargeant Sammy Baker, Mickey Walker, Fred Apostoli, and Billy Conn at Kezar and old Dreamland.

Finally, he got a shot at champion Jackie Fields at Seals Stadium. February 22 (a favorite Bay Area fight date), 1933, Corbett landed the first punch and was all over Fields, dancing inside and out, flashing lefts and rights and making a whirlwind finish in the tenth. Ref Navy Jack Kennedy, then trying out his new ten-point-per-round scoring system, gave Corbett the decision by a wide margin.

The standing-room-only crowd went wild. Jabs had closed Corbett's right eye, but he was now world welterweight champ, a much-coveted crown in those days. His friends urged him to take a few breather fights and capitalize on his title, but he didn't heed the advice and signed for a title go with the hard-banging McLarnin. As champ Corbett could call the tune and friends hoped he'd make San Francisco the scene, but he chose Los Angeles.

The fight was ballyhooed as the Super Bowl would be today. The date was May 30, 1933. McLarnin showered blows from the opening bell and finally came in with a vicious, looping right that landed on Corbett's jaw like hammer of Thor. Corbett went down for the count short of two minutes. Bay Area radio listeners couldn't believe their ears, for Corbett was hard to hit. His unorthodox left-handed style made him stand out like a Lefty Grove or Gomez on the mound. Small wonder his followers were in a state of shock.

Corbett had lost his hard-won title only ninety-five days after winning it. He never regained it. McLarnin wouldn't fight him again. The loser had entered the ring with a flu fever of 101° but never uttered a word of alibi. No excuses were really needed, though, for McLarnin, born in Ireland, was one of the great welterweights in history. In the 1930s he beat legendary Lou Ambers, Benny Leonard, Tony Cazoneri, and Barney Ross, winning two or three fights against the latter.

Corbett had nothing but bad luck after his ring days ended. First off, he was mugged by thugs in a Chicago World's Fair parking lot and spent days in a hospital. Later he went through the windshield in a bad car mishap and hovered between life and death.

But the worst was yet to come. He became affected with Alzheimer's disease, a form of senility with no known cure. Though still physically fit at eighty, he couldn't recognize his wife, who came daily to the care home.

One-round kayos are rare indeed. Louis is generally regarded as the first-round knocker-outer champ among the big men. The bigger they are, the harder (and sometimes sooner) they fall. He got crackin' in his first pro fight, flattening Jack Kracken in less than a minute. All told he scored a dozen first-round kayos. Among his victims were Buddy Baer, John Henry Lewis, and Jack Roper.

Jack Dempsey was no slouch at ending fights in canto numero uno. He scored about fifty of them, but most came in exhibitions against stiffs. His legitimate victims, however, included Fireman Jim Flynn, Freddy Fulton, Carl Morris, and Canuck Arthur Pelkey.

One shouldn't overlook Rocky Marciano, who could hit as hard with his elbows as his fists. Eight of his first ten pro opponents bit the dust in the first round, but Rocky tailed off as he went up in class. Max Baer, maybe the hardest hitter of them all, scored thirteen first-round kayos.

What was the shortest fight of all time? There are several claimants, but the one most recognized is Eddie Murdock, who came out of his corner, shook hands with Willie Siegel, and belted him out with the first punch. Elapsed time: eleven seconds.

What about the longest fight in ring annals? Nat Fleischer, a walking encyclopedia for digging up ring oddities, claims it was a 110-rounder between Andy Bowen and Jack Burke in New Orleans. It lasted seven hours, nineteen minutes, and was called a draw when the referee determined neither man could continue. Bowen had a mania for getting into boxathons. The very next month it took him eighty-five rounds to put Jack Everhard away.

One of Fleischer's "most unusuals" was two opponents knocking each other out with simultaneous punches in the fourth round. The ref called it a draw. Another oddity concerns Dempsey's one-time manager, Doc Kearns. Seems he once had a fighter, Battling Billy Braton, who broke a hand before a fight. Rather than lose the $150 purse, Kearns not only fought one Jolly Roger Smith but knocked him galley west for a kayo.

Archie Moore: Mongoose's Memories

OLD-TIMERS, and even young-timers, remember Archie Moore, one of the great boxers of his day. "The Mongoose," as he is often called, hasn't changed much. I hadn't seen or heard from him for some time until just before sitting down to write this. Moore still has a photographic memory of his 251 fights (give or take a couple), more than half of which he won by knockouts, mostly with his effective left hook.

He tips the scales at 210 to 215, a bit over his fighting weight of 173. Nobody ever shed weight or added it faster than Moore. After a fight he'd "slop up" and put on 30 pounds, then take it off just as quickly before his next fight.

More recently, he lost by kayo to a hive of bees, which he maintains as a hobby at his San Diego home. An amateur bee-keeper, he was moving a hive in his backyard when the bees attacked him. He was stung worse than Muhammad Ali (then Cassius Clay) stung him in the fourth round of their fight, in the days when Clay boasted he would "float like a butterfly and sting like a bee."

They rushed Moore to the hospital. He nearly lost his life, but is as good as new again. "It was the worst fight of my career," says Moore, who hasn't lost his humor.

Moore doesn't begrudge today's ring men their big paydays. "They're making it big in all other sports; why not boxing?" he says. "I'm not bitter, but I'm not forgetting either that I didn't get a title shot until I fought pro for thirteen years, and when

I did, I got only six thousand dollars for my end after winning the light heavy title from Joey Maxim in St. Louis (in December 1952). I had to borrow ten thousand dollars to get out of town."

Moore was as sharp and alert as ever as he gave us some of his "bests," including the answer to who hit him the hardest of all his opponents over twenty-nine years, a career which began against the Poco Kid when Moore was only twenty in Hot Springs, Arkansas, and ended with his final fight against Nap Mitchel of Michigan City, Indiana, in 1965. He won both fights by knockout.

I fully expected Moore to say Rocky Marciano hit the hardest, but no—it was Yvon Durelle. "I've been hit hard by a lot of guys," he began, though he was no punching bag. "And I've been knocked out as the result of a series of softening punches. But for one punch, one blockbuster, Durelle hit the hardest when he knocked me down three times in the first round. His first punch was the hardest I ever took."

That one was in the Montreal Forum. "I never dreamed I could be hit so hard," Moore says, adding that he derived more satisfaction from fighting Durelle than from any other fight, including the one in which he knocked down Marciano. "Only thing about that one is, Rocky got up," Moore quipped.

"I'll always remember my fight with Durelle as my finest hour in the ring, because after he knocked me down four times all told, I staggered back and knocked him out in the eleventh. I proved myself."

In his three decades as a pro, Moore says the only bad beating he ever took was from Marciano. I covered that fight for the heavyweight title in Yankee Stadium. When I saw Moore in the dressing room after the fight, he had a lump over his right eye about as big as an egg, but his first words were, "I'd like to fight him again."

In that one, Moore might have won the heavyweight crown,

but we thought he let Rocky off the hook by being too slow to follow up on his knockdown. "I floored him in the second round," Moore recalls. I remember it as either the third or fourth, but Moore should know.

"It was a hard fight for us both," adds Moore. "I blame the ref, Harry Kessler," he said, without noticeable bitterness. "He got excited. He escorted me to a neutral corner, then wasted time getting back and wiping the resin off Marciano's gloves. I can't forgive him for that."

After the fifth round, Marciano knocked Moore down six times. Some still call Marciano an "elbow puncher."

"But," said Moore, "you better believe it, he could hit." Kessler wanted to stop the fight after the sixth knockdown, but my corner wouldn't agree."

Admitting the big paydays in the ring today bedazzle him, Moore insisted several times that he isn't jealous, merely envious. "What is missing in the ring today is that the contestants don't know how to pace themselves. I learned to, early, and that's why I lasted so long. The lack of rating themselves is amazing. Bill Shoemaker and Johnny Longden made great reps as jockeys because they could pace themselves, but fighters today are too gung ho. They want to go all out from the start."

Moore says the best all-round opponent he ever met was probably middleweight Charley Burley. But there were also Lloyd Marshall and Eddie Booker. "I'm talking now about all-around ring artists, fellows with all the skills that I fought. It would be close between those three."

Moore says he treasures memories of some of his Bay Area fights—against Bob Dunlop, Jack Chase, Tiger Waite, Marshall, and Jimmy Casino, whom he fought for promoter Jimmy Murray.

In all, he was to participate in twenty-six title fights. The record books have him scoring 127 knockouts, although by his own count it was 138. But what are a few kayos more or less to a guy with as many as Moore scored?

Moore's birthdate is also in dispute. The *Ring Record Book* says he was born in December, 1916, which would have him closing in on seventy. But a St. Louis birth certificate has him at seventy-three. Neither Moore nor his wife Joan will tell. He fought as an amateur welterweight before turning pro in 1936. From then on, he fought in the middleweight, light heavyweight, and heavyweight divisions.

Besides his beehive hobby, Moore has been busy working with boys in an urban-development program; he remains as a ringside regular at San Diego fights.

In face, taking a leaf out of the book of his one-time manager, Jack Kearns, Moore is ever on the lookout for a heavyweight prospect he can tutor and manage to a world title. His latest find is seven-foot-one Ed Payne. So far Payne, though endowed with the coordination most string bean–tall men like six-foot-six Primo Carnera lacked, has yet to prove he doesn't possess a glass jaw.

Many boxing pundits rate Moore as the best light heavyweight champion in boxing history. The division was established eighty years ago, conceived with the idea that a grade should be established to include men between the middleweight class (then set at 158 pounds) and such big guys as Jim Jeffries (who scaled at 215). Since then, some great light heavyweight champions have reigned: Georges Carpentier, Gene Tunney, Battling Levinsky, Mike McTigue, Melio Bettina, Freddie Mills, Ezzard Charles, and Gus Lesnevich.

Willie Hoppe,
Superstar of Billiards

WILLIE HOPPE, world's billiard champion, belongs on any list of sports superstars. He died in 1959 in Florida at the age of seventy-one after being world renowned as Mr. Billiards for almost half a century. He was the only champion to outdistance all the sports crown–holders of his day—Dempsey, Ruth, Bobby Jones, et al.

Willie won his last world title in San Francisco in 1952, seven years before he died. I covered the matches staged at the 924 Club on Market Street, a place owned by Welker Cochran, himself a one-time balkline champion.

When Hoppe won his first world title, Ty Cobb was just blossoming as a .300 hitter, Christy Mathewson and Walter Johnson were in their primes, Jim Thorpe was leading the Carlisle Indians to grid fame, Walter Eckersall was quarterbacking for Chicago University, and Willie Heston was at Michigan.

Hoppe outlasted them all by many years. He won his title at fifteen years of age, defeating the great French artist, Maurice Vignaux—"the Old Lion," as Paris called him. Sitting in the gallery rooting for him were Willie's pals, Nat Goodwin, Eddie Foy, and Tod Sloan. This was in 1906.

In the finals of the San Francisco title match of 1952, Hoppe beat Herb Hardt, a young Chicago bank clerk who had taken his vacation hoping to find Hoppe "all through" and to dethrone him. Willie was sixty-four at the time and gave young Hardt a billiard lesson he'd never forget.

I went to lunch with Hoppe the next day when he announced he would retire from competitive billiards. He did so a few months later, but continued giving exhibitions. "Billiards can use new faces," he told me. "People are tired of seeing one guy at the top so many years. A spectacular young new player will revive the game."

Willie doubted if the present generation would work as hard as he had to become and stay a champ. He never did learn to drive a car, fearing it might stiffen his pliant wrists. He shunned movies lest they irritate his eyes, never smoked, and never took a drink until he was forty.

He came to San Francisco for a long visit just after he retired. A neat, white-haired man, trim and healthy-looking, he walked into my office at the *Call Bulletin* with a brisk step. He still hadn't put away the magic cue he had wielded for so many years. He was playing exhibitions, nearly all of which were in the winter, for he was an avid baseball fan and didn't want to be shackled to a cue when the fragrance of horsehide was in the air.

Speaking in his quiet, precise tone amid memories few sports personalities could match, he said he had enjoyed it all, and was proudest of winning his world title the first time he competed for it and defending it successfully forty-six years later.

"But I can't stand the strain anymore," he said, "I can't concentrate on shots as I could when I was younger. Not in competition. I'm all right if I punish myself, but the nerves require too much conscious effort. Those last matches were too much for me. I finished a bundle of nerves."

He had appeared outwardly calm in winning this last title in San Francisco, but he confessed that inside he had butterflies. "To pinpoint my way through a three-cushion billiard title match would take more than I have."

Hoppe mentioned that being a champion entailed hours of hard work. He practiced endlessly to improve himself. And the hours he spent over a billiard table were only part of it. He lived as a boxer might while training for a big bout—going to bed early, getting up early, hitting the road, and living on a rigid diet. He checked his weight daily. He was strong, tough, and fit when the big tournaments came and he took his cue in hand to make the ivory ball jump through a hoop.

In scanning my old notes on his last world title match, I find Willie had gotten his fifty points to Hardt's twenty-six in forty-four frames. Hoppe was slow to warm up. His young opponent got a hot run of five billiards in the eleventh inning. This put him ahead 8-6. If this nettled the suave, poker-faced Hoppe, nobody in the gallery sensed it.

While trailing this early, Willie didn't even give his young opponent the satisfaction of looking on as he made his shots. Instead, he sat gazing at the ceiling nonchalantly and recalling, perhaps, the years he had spent around dingy, smoke-filled pool halls.

In contrast to Hardt, who figured each shot carefully, taking over a minute to decide on his angle, Hoppe had his little diamond-shaped spots on the sides and ends of the table. Rarely did he take more than twenty seconds between shots. He got his angle quickly and just blazed away.

The first twenty-seven innings found him shooting below his usual par, which was better than a billiard per inning. Then in the twenty-eighth inning, he got in his first big run—four. This gave him a 28-15 lead, but he didn't begin to widen till the thirty-sixth frame when he got in a run of five. This was the turning point. He began to pull away. His cue work of the last twelve frames was that of a champion, missing only once in those final twelve.

Only once did Hoppe exhibit tension. In the forty-first inning, when ahead 45-26, his cue ball stopped dead at what looked like a distance of less than an eighth of an inch from completing a score. Referee Joe Sebastian ruled it no score. Hoppe shot him an icy look and returned to his chair.

Willie admitted to playing under his best in the opening rounds. "The cloth on the table was new and a bit thick," he explained. "The ball slid a lot. And the dark shade of the red ball bothered me. We use a lighter color in the East. It's easier to see. The darker one affected my accuracy. I guess I'm getting a little blind."

But he endeared himself to me when he added, "Don't mind the alibis. Billiard players are worse alibi artists than golfers. If they get beat, either the table or the balls were no good, somebody coughed just as they were making their shot, their opponent didn't leave them anything to hit, or he was lucky to have made so many unconscious shots."

As he talked, he affectionately stroked the 18-ounce, 55 1/2-inch maple cue he had used for nearly fifty years. His dad, a barber in New York City, had given it to him just before Willie had sailed for Europe to meet the crafty Vignaux and beat him for the title. There had been a billiard table in back of his dad's barbershop, where Willie had started playing when he wasn't even tall enough to reach over the table without standing on a soapbox.

Just after he defeated Hardt, the challenger said, as if surprised, "Say, that Hoppe fellow is rather amazing!" Willie's opponents had been saying that about him for nearly fifty years, ever since he became the Boy Wonder champion.

The Kentucky Derby Is Short, But Memories Last Forever

OF ALL THE big national sports events I've covered, the Kentucky Derby is number one as the most glamorous. Not even a World Series, Super Bowl, or heavyweight title fight can match it for thrills and excitement.

It is the oldest continuously run stakes in America, going back to 1875. The race itself lasts only two minutes, but memories of it can endure a lifetime, including those of incidents leading up to and following what Bill Corum first called "the Run for the Roses."

Dogwood, azaleas, and tulips are exploding in color when America's top three-year-olds prance out on the track en route to post and the band strikes up "My Old Kentucky Home," and one needn't be a native hardboot to feel one's spine tingling way down deep.

What if Stephen Foster, the lyrical songwriter, never was in Kentucky in his life, as some contend? It matters not. The song savors as genuine as the taste of a real mint julep made by a native Louisville matron. It stirs the heartstrings far more than "Maryland, My Maryland," symbolic of the Preakness, or "Sidewalks of New York," theme song of the Belmont. Few opening lines of American ballads stir the depths of the heart more than "the sun shines bright."

Almost as fascinating as the race is a visit to the barns on the backstretch all Derby week to chat with owners, trainers, riders, and stablehands for the latest gossip before the race—

and post mortems after it. Birds chatter in the barn eaves and the grass outside actually looks blue as the dew sparkles in the early morning sun.

Only three California-breds have won the classic—Morvich, Swaps, and Decidedly—a sad commentary for the number one horse-race state in the United States (but not number one in racehorses). Kentucky (who else?) leads in Derby winners with eighty-three. Florida has had four; Virginia, California, and Tennessee, three each; Texas and New Jersey, two; with one each for Missouri, Ohio, Illinois, Kansas, and Montana. Four were foreigners—Canada and England, two each.

While a potent California threat would add spice to the race, the Derby is still America's number one horse classic, and to many, its top sports thrill, with a genuine mint julep thrown in on the side. Some year a horse named Mint Julep will win the race and that will be the ultimate, for the julep is to the Derby what peanuts, popcorn, and Cracker Jacks are to baseball.

I've often been asked to name the "bests" of the twenty-six derbies I covered from the Churchill Downs scene. The most exciting and glamorous winner had to be Whirlaway, 1941. The way he flew up the stretch sent my pulse throbbing as if Mexican jumping beans were playing leapfrog inside me. How that Triple Crowner flew in the final quarter! He was going so fast turning to enter that long stretch, I thought he'd go right through the fence. And he carried his own "flag"—a plumed tail that reached nearly to the ground and stuck straight out when he turned on speed.

The greatest Derby come-from-behinders were Ponder, 1949; Needles, 1956; and Carry Back, 1961. Carry Back was probably the best ground closer. He entered the stretch 13.5 lengths behind and won it.

The hot wire-to-wire speed burner of my time was War Admiral, 1937. He shook off every horse that made a run at him and four did, one at a time—at the first turn, on the back side, on the far turn, and down the home stretch. Charley Kurtsinger, who lived only a block from the track, stayed in front, waving at his wife and kids as he passed the house.

I'd have to call Citation the best horse I ever saw win the Derby, although the fact that he became the first to win one million dollars in purses may have influenced me.

Who was the greatest trainer? It had to be Plain Ben Jones. He saddled the most Derby winners (six)—Lawrin, Whirlaway, Pensive, Citation, Ponder, and Hill Gail—and helped his son Jimmie win with Tim Tam and Iron Liege. Trainers play a bigger role in winning the Derby than in most stakes because of the distance and the difficult, cuppy track. It takes a dead-fit steed to win this 1.25-mile test of stamina.

I can see Plain Ben in my mind's eye now, sitting a stable pony, watching Ponder cooling out after a morning gallop. "You have to bring your Derby winner to his peak not yesterday or tomorrow, but today," he said. "Timing is of the essence."

In that derby, Ponder was lying dead last at the three-quarters pole, but closed like a jet to wear down the capable Capot.

And who was the best Derby jockey? This is one race in which the still-great Bill Shoemaker tried to dominate but failed. He has ridden in twenty-four Derbies and brought home four winners. It might have been five, but Shoe misjudged the finish line in 1957 astride Gallant Man and blew the race to Iron Liege.

Eddie Arcaro is the true king of the Derby winners. He rode in twenty-one (three less than Shoe) and won five, tying Bill Hartack. Eddie was only nineteen when he won his first, aboard Lawrin, 1938, and I recall a story he told on himself about that race. Seems he was a kid full of adventure.

"I went out on the town Derby eve," he related. "Didn't get in much before sunrise, but I figured I could sleep all day as Derby time wasn't until after five in the afternoon.

"But about seven in the morning, trainer Ben Jones phoned me in my hotel room and ordered me out to the track 'right away.' He sent a taxi. I got to the barn heavy-headed with juleps. Mr. Jones about walked my legs off, taking me every inch of the way around the strip, showing me how deep it was down by the rail and pointing out some paths where the track was firmer.

" 'Now, son,' he told me, 'no matter what happens, stay off that rail.' When Lawrin hit the first turn he had only one horse beat. Only chance I had to win was to save ground on the rail. So I stayed there, the shortest way around, and was still there when we whizzed by the front runners to win going away. In the winner's circle I heard Ben telling reporters, 'Arcaro's my boy. He rode Lawrin just the way I told him to.' "

Shoe Turns 50 and Looks Back over a Great Career

IT SEEMS LIKE no more than yesterday that an unknown eighteen-year-old apprentice rider scored the first win of his career aboard Shafter V at Golden Gate Fields. That was back in 1949. When Bill Shoemaker celebrated his fiftieth birthday, he had ridden more horses into the win circle than any jockey ever dreamed was possible—more than 8,000 victories. The Shoe just kept winning and winning, and about everything came up roses for him.

Is Bill (he prefers Bill to Willie) still America's leading rider at the half-century milestone? Not if you figure his annual crop of victories. Lafitte Pincay and Chris McCarron are the top two. The Shoe could perhaps match them, but the price of pressing would be too costly at his age.

Just call him still the best stakes rider of them all. When a big-money race is on, owners and trainers who want to be sure they win with the best horse send for Shoe. He's still tops in the hundred granders.

Johnny Longden rode until he was fifty-nine and went out a winner aboard George Royal at Santa Anita in 1966. Can the Shoe last nine more years? Probably, but he won't. He hasn't made the final decision on the date he's going to hang up his tack, but he implies it will be long before he's fifty-nine.

He is still a top rider but, unlike Pete Rose, Gaylord Perry, and other slaves to statistics, he has no zest to compile them. Three, four, at the most five, mounts a day are enough for him. This isn't enough to make him competitive with Pincay and McCarron for the most annual wins. "My wife (Cindy) and daughter (eight-year-old Amanda) mean more to me than all the winners I ever rode or ever will," he said at Del Mar one day.

He rarely rides two-year-olds anymore. "They are too hard to manage," he says. He wants older, more tractable mounts. And he won't let his agent, Harry Silbert, who has been with him for more than thirty years, accept mounts on cheap horses or ones unsteady on their pins. He's through taking chances and going through narrow openings in a race.

Recently Shoemaker took himself off all his mounts for the day. He says he fell asleep on the beach while acquiring a suntan on a Tuesday, when there's no racing, and acquired an acute sunburn. The Shoe would never have done that in his youth.

A few days later he scored a triple, then chalked up another triple a few days after that. "Some days they come in bunches," he offered. "I ride day by day and concentrate on just one race at a time."

Still, he says, not too many things about racing concern him anymore. He's wrapped up in his family. That's why I give him no more than another year in the saddle before he quits altogether. He has ridden millions of dollars worth of stakes winners and has plenty of money, though he is not as rich as many think. Married three times, he gave his second wife a whale of a big settlement. But he has a big home in Arcadia in the shadows of Santa Anita and enough money to live in style the rest of his life.

Shoemaker isn't the shy boy he was his first few years around racetracks when they called him Silent Shoe. But he is still modest. "Harry (Silbert) always did get me good, live mounts to ride," he says, explaining his success.

True, his agent did just that. But the Shoe had a lot more

than just a good agent. His ability to rate a horse was and still is uncanny. He "feels" when a horse wants to run, and he sits back and waits until that moment comes. Nothing excites him during the running of a race. If he gets in a tight spot, he stays calm until he gets clear and there's racing room. He rarely goes to the whip, unless a horse starts loafing on him. Horses run kindly for him. It's incredible the way he times his move on a stretch runner, and it is usually a gradual but steady move.

He isn't perfect. He lost a Kentucky Derby in 1950 because he misjudged the finish line, eased Gallant Man up thinking the race was over and lost by a nose to Iron Liege. He has often chided me for not letting him forget that slip.

Only a handful of baseball players got as many as three thousand hits lifetime, and not too many jockeys rode that many either—the English jockey Gordon Richards, and American booters Eddie Arcaro, Ted Atkinson, Johnny Adams, Ralph Neves, and Longden. Shoe outshone all these illustrious predecessors, and he was the youngest when he did it. He succeeded Longden as the world's winningest jockey. Johnny had 6,033 lifetime wins when he quit riding. Shoemaker, with nearly 8,050 as this is written, has become the Ty Cobb of the jockey world. Okay, make it "the Pete Rose."

Yet he has never won an Athlete of the Year Award. More is the pity! No jockey has been accorded this honor because most sportswriters refuse to recognize jockeys, claiming they do not qualify as athletes. I will argue to my dying day that this is not the case.

Webster's defines an athlete as "a person trained or fit to contest in exercises requiring physical ability and/or stamina." This definition seems especially suited to the men who race. Particularly from a rider's standpoint, horse racing is surely competitive. Racing requires a strong pair of hands, split-second timing, physical strength (particularly when it comes to applying the whip), competitive spirit, perfect conditioning, a great sense of daring and courage, and balance (it takes a great sense of balance for a 110-pounder to wrestle a 1,200-pound horse around the track). If these attributes do not add up to *Webster's* definition of an athlete, then I must be off my rocker.

A jockey can't always ride a race exactly as instructed in the paddock. He has to think and act at the same time. An alert mind is essential, and the Shoe certainly has one. He knows there's always a move to make and when to make it. You can't mull it over. If you do, the opening is gone.

Longden, who lost his lead to Shoemaker in 1970, points to another asset of the Shoe. "He always plays it cool," Longden says, without a trace of rancor toward the rider who passed him. "I honestly believe his even disposition is Shoemaker's greatest asset. Oh, he has all the rest—he's a good judge of pace, has perfect hands, and is a good size. But if you stop to think about it, you never saw him blow a race because of a temper."

All these things add up to the winningest jockey of them all, who has ridden over eighty-five million dollars worth of purse monies into the win circle.

Showing that his native state considers jockeys athletes, Shoemaker was named to the Texas Sports Hall of Fame. He's from Fabian, in the western part of Texas.

Longden Got His Start
Riding a Mule

JOCKEYS CAN TRACE their inspiration to become race riders to many an incident or whim, but Johnny Longden's has to be about the most bizarre of any. He got the horseback-riding bug by riding a mule pulling cars in a Canadian coal mine when he was only thirteen years old. This started him daydreaming and carried him to fame as a jockey for forty years, his riding career ending with 6,032 wins.

It was a world mark later bettered by Bill Shoemaker who, ironically, was his "presenter" at the annual Bay Area Sports Hall of Fame dinner February 21, 1984, at San Francisco's St. Francis Hotel.

Johnny is the first racetracker to make the Hall of Fame. It isn't easy for a jockey to get in because of a mistaken notion on the parts of many media voters that a jockey doesn't qualify as an athlete, though it takes as much skill, timing, competitive urge, and sportsmanship to reach the top of this profession as it does in baseball, football, or most any sport.

Since a jockey is finally to be admitted this year (along with Alice Marble, Leo Nomellini, Gino Marchetti, and the late Buck Shaw), why wasn't Shoemaker chosen? After all, he rode his very first winner at Golden Gate Fields. Perhaps because Shoe rarely rode in the Bay Area, while Longden was a regular at Bay Meadows and Golden Gate Fields. Indeed, he rode at old Tanforan way back in 1931.

Johnny was born in Wales. The family, almost destitute,

156

moved to Taber, Alberta, where he joined his father down in the mines and developed a liking for animals, soon getting a job herding cows on horseback. This led to riding races at small fairs in Western Canada.

His first official winner on a recognized track was in Salt Lake City, aboard a steed with the unromantic name Hugo K. Asher, a nine-year-old gelding worth about three hundred dollars. The track operator was Bill Kyne, later boss at Bay Meadows.

It was rough sledding for Longden at first, but he saved enough to buy a hay-burner named Trossachs for eight hundred dollars and headed for Tanforan. There was no stall space available, but the Southern Pacific Railroad let him stable in an unused boxcar. Johnny slept with his horse.

One Bill Hartman gave him his first big break, putting him up on Bahamas for the California Breeders' Handicap. It was Longden's first stakes win. There was very little racing in the West in those days. Hartman shipped Bahamas to Tijuana with Longden for a race against the great Phar Lap, maybe the fastest horse in the world.

Recalling that race, Johnny said, "I led the field to the three-eighths pole when Phar Lap went by all of us like we were standing still. He was just a blur. All I saw of him was his hind end down the home stretch."

Longden says Count Fleet was the best horse he ever rode. He won the 1942 Kentucky Derby on him, as well as the Preakness and Belmont for the Triple Crown triumph. Years later I asked him, "Wasn't Noor a better race horse?"

Johnny replied, "No. But second best. After all, Noor beat Citation four times."

Longden was aboard in all four. Citation was the first race-horse to earn a million in purses. Two of those four races were at Golden Gate and they were probably the greatest turf duels ever staged in the Bay Area. Three of the wins were world records at the time. Charlie "Seabiscuit" Howard bought Noor, a big, rangy Irish-bred, from the Aga Khan, and brought him to the United States in 1949.

Johnny was noted for winning races by stealing a big early lead, but he could come from behind, too. Noor was a long strider and began slowly, then would close like a rocket.

Asked to compare Noor and Count Fleet, Longden said, "They were completely different. Court Fleet was rough and headstrong. Noor had an even disposition, gentle and kindly. Both were honest but had their own ways of getting home on top. Noor was easy to ride, Count Fleet often hard to handle."

Other great horses Longden rode included Whirlaway, Top Row, Swaps, Round Table, and Louis B. Mayer's great filly, Busher. Among the great trainers who used him were Pinky Grimes, George Odom, Willie Molter, and Tom Smith.

The greatest ride I ever saw Johnny make was in 1951 in the Santa Anita Handicap aboard Moonrush, when he all but carried him across the finish line. The field was strung out like a long freight train, with only two horses in contention a sixteenth from the wire. Moonrush had led all the way to that point, when suddenly Next Move passed him. It looked for all the world like the Vanderbilt horse would be an easy winner, but Moonrush came again.

If ever a race was won by the jockey, this was it. Longden had psyched Eric Guerin on Next Move into thinking Moonrush was chucking it due to the too-sizzling pace, then Johnny rode the daylights out of his mount to win by a neck.

One of Johnny's early agents was Joe Hernandez, later to become famous as the Santa Anita race caller. But his long-time agent was Basil Smith. For years they were inseparable. "He was the greatest agent I ever knew, could smell out a live mount a mile away, and he had good contacts," Longden explains. "The only reason we broke up was he put me on eight mounts a day at an age when I needed to slow down. I wanted to take things a little easy."

Longden had short legs and arms and was nicknamed "the Pumper" because he liked to be out in front early. He had to resort to the sweatbox as much as many riders. For most of his career he rode at around 112 pounds. When he had to carry extra weight, he used a money belt with slugs of lead in it. Most jockeys use a special vest.

Johnny ended his riding career in a blaze of glory by riding the horse George Royal when he won the classic San Juan Capistrano at Santa Anita in March 1966. He was fifty-nine when he hung up his tack. This race was a 1.5 miler and the last of the 32,407 races he rode in. He had been riding for over forty years. Johnny won out in a life-and-death stretch duel with Plaque, trained by Laz Barrera.

He got every ounce of stamina out of George Royal; it was a storybook ending to a great jockey's career. The win tempted him to go on riding, but Johnny decided it was a good way to go out. His career record of 6,023 wins stood until Shoemaker passed him in 1970.

Abandoning such an active life proved boring, so Johnny became a trainer (and a most successful one) with horses owned by him and Calgary horsemen. His crowning achievement as a trainer was winning the 1969 Kentucky Derby by a neck with Majestic Prince.

"Give Longden credit, not me," said Bill Hartack, the winning jockey.

Majestic Prince became the first undefeated horse to win the Derby since Morvich in 1922, and Longden became the first to win in both as a jockey and as a trainer.

Byron Nelson, Golf Legend

ONCE ON THE circuit, most pro golfers get it in their blood and, being no different in this respect from boxers, baseballers, or grid warriors of pro vintage, can't quit at their peak. There have been few exceptions—Byron Nelson is a notable one. Unlike many, he knew when to put the putter away. Bobby Jones tired of competition at twenty-eight and retired from active campaigning; Walter Hagen won the British Open at thirty-six and that was about the last one saw of him as a top-runger. Nelson was satisfied to be kingpin for eight years, from 1939 through 1947, and at the age of thirty-five limited his campaigning for the next five years to a couple of big tournaments a year, including the Crosby at Monterey.

Sports lore is replete with Olympian feats, superhuman efforts such as Joe DiMaggio's fifty-six-game hitting streak, Ruth's sixty homers in 144 games, Bob Beamon's twenty-nine-foot long jump and Mark Spitz's seven gold medals. But even after more than thirty years, it is still hard to grasp the immensity of Nelson's winning eleven consecutive PGA golf tournaments. Johnny Miller won three in a row in 1974 and created a whirl of excitement on the tour by winning five more that year.

To put things in perspective, Jack Nicklaus, whom many think was the greatest of the 1970s, has never won more than seven in a season. Tom Weiskopf won five of eight in one 1973 stretch in which he had twenty of forty rounds in the 60s. Golf people called it the hot streak to end all hot streaks.

Yet Nelson's feat of eleven in a row in 1945, when he was a familiar figure on Northern California courses, remains unbelievable. He won eighteen tournaments that year. Statistics show he was an unparalleled shot maker. He averaged 68-plus strokes for forty rounds of the PGA tour. He played nineteen consecutive rounds in under 70, and his competitive quality is shown by a 67-plus average for his closing rounds.

They always said Nelson was one top-flighter who could have gone on forever, because he didn't have a nerve in his body. They called him the mechanical man of the game because he never seemed to have to key himself up for any particular event. He just hit 'em as they came without wasting nervous energy. Nor did he leave his good shots on the practice course. When he competed in the San Francisco Open in 1947, he confined himself to a couple of warm-up swings and a visit to the greens to get the feel of them with his putting stick.

Some said Nelson quit to escape the threat of Ben Hogan and Sam Snead, who had just come back from World War II. But he had beaten both consistently before, so this hardly holds water.

All the great ones have their best shots. Nelson was, of course, good at all of them, but he was really king of the long irons—the number 1, 2, and 3 clubs. Those are the three clubs I always tried to keep in my bag because they'd never go straight. They'd wind around like a pretzel, then go in the rough. Perhaps it was this that made me admire Nelson more than any of his time.

He was so amazingly accurate with his iron shots they had to be seen to be believed. One quip that was current about the time he said good-bye to the competitive circuit in 1942 was that he just got tired of hitting shots and finding his ball in the divot he had made on his previous round.

It was during the Crosby at Pebble Beach in 1953 that I asked the late Freddy Corcoran, long-time tournament chairman of the PGA, to name a mythical composite best golfer of the modern age up to that time. Who were his "bests?" Off the tee for distance, Sam Snead; accuracy, Jim Turnesa; mudder, Dr. Cary Middlecoff; trap shots and chipping, Julius Boros; iron play, Byron Nelson (with Jimmy Demaret next); putting under pressure, a standoff between Jackie Burke, Jr., and Lloyd Mangrum.

After Byron retired, Corky said he could have gone on for ten more years as a top-bracket swinger. "His mental attitude was always the finest of any champion I've known in sports. To begin with, he never considered himself the champion he was when he wore the crown. He was so modest he couldn't understand why he stood out above the field. He attributed his success more to luck. But, take it from me, luck plays only a small part, for Nelson possessed that unique combination of physical skill and temperament that is rare, but once you have it you become unbeatable."

Nelson wasn't a great putter. "He doesn't have to be," Corky countered. "When you can pitch 'em right up there to the flag as he does, there needn't be any three putts on any green."

Somehow, Nelson matured earlier than Hogan and coincidentally, reached the age at which he chose to retire at the same time Hogan was just starting his period of greatness.

Oddly enough, while Hogan and Nelson were contemporaries (and Texas ones at that), their careers never managed to precipitate too many showdowns. One was in the Los Angeles Open, when Hogan won by five strokes at the Riviera course. I watched the first nine holes of that one and then moseyed out to the Santa Anita racetrack. I wrote about what I had done in my column the next day and a reader wrote in that he was stopping his subscription because I had deserted a top golf match for a horse race!

Budge's Booming Backhand

DON BUDGE, "the Redhead," dominated tennis in his day, the years just prior to World War II. His backhand stroke was the most powerful of his time. Many regarded him as greater than Bill Tilden. Indeed, this argument often rages to this day.

Six feet tall, flaming-haired, freckled, and with a pleasing personality, Don was born in Oakland in 1916. He inherited athletic ability from his dad, a Scotsman, who had starred in soccer for the Glasgow Rangers before emigrating to the United States. The elder Budge had a laundry business in Oakland and also owned and managed a semipro baseball club.

Like his dad, Don liked baseball and had aspirations to become a major leaguer, but his older brother, Lloyd, convinced him he should forget baseball—that he was destined to become the greatest tennis player of his time.

The Redhead was king of tennis from 1937 till World War II. A good friend of mine, Merv Griffin, Sr., father of Merv the television talk show star, once told me Budge was the best junior player in California in his early teens. I saw him play only once and was impressed with his fine court appearance, dressed in long flannels, white shoes, and a white Davis Cup blazer. He looked like the champion he was.

I can recall vividly how, in 1937, he thrilled America with his big upset win over Baron Gottfried von Cramm from Germany. This victory brought the Davis Cup back to America for the first time in a decade.

And the great match had political overtones. So anxious was Adolf Hitler to have von Cramm beat Budge that he telephoned the baron in the Wimbledon dressing room just before the match and gave him a pep talk.

The führer never forgave von Cramm for losing. Hitler had suffered great loss of pride the year before when Jesse Owens had made a shambles of the best runners and jumpers of the "master race" in the Berlin Olympics.

The pressure Hitler put on von Cramm was terrific. Budge always said that this match, with Queen Mary looking on, was the greatest net duel he was ever in. "I never played better, nor did I ever play anyone as good as von Cramm was that day," he later opined.

The first two sets went to von Cramm. Budge won the next two, and eight match points later won the match. Experts rated the German's forehand superior, while Budge's backhand and serve were better. Budge and von Cramm remained good friends.

After the match, Wally Pate, Davis Cup captain, said "no other tennis player, living or dead, could have beaten either man this day." Strong words.

Budge was to leave the amateur ranks at twenty-three. The pros tried to sign him the year before, offering him a guaranteed fifty thousand dollars per year, financial security for life in those days. But Budge said he wanted to repay amateur tennis for all it had done for him and to stick around for awhile to help defend the newly won Davis Cup. This made a big hit with the brass, and enabled Budge to leave the amateur ranks with no recriminations.

In his last year as an amateur (1938), Budge scored the only grand slam in men's tennis, up till then, by winning the American, Australian, French, and British titles—the world's four major crowns. And, except against the French, he won without undue stress or strain. This caused sportswriters to vote him the top athlete—amateur or pro—of 1938. He also won the Sullivan Award in 1937, the first tennis player to do it.

Budge had a dynamic serve. He'd come up to his full height on his first serve. His second was almost as hard as the first.

The late Jim Moffet of San Francisco, a bosom friend of mine who started the Youth Tennis Foundation, once gave me an appraisal of Budge. "Many thought him less graceful than some of the players he easily beat," he began. "But when he was in form he had no weakness. He didn't like to take the net behind his serve. Being a good athlete he could do it, but it wasn't his style. He wasn't the scurrying, scrambling type. He preferred to come in only for the kill."

What about his backhand? Was it really a world-beater? "It was murderous," said Moffet, "the most famed ground stroke in tennis. His opponents sometimes misjudged its speed because he had a way of sliding forward and stepping into the ball, which increased the speed of impact, even when his racquet hardly seemed to swing at all.

"His backhand had real flair, that great freedom of motion which made it the envy of every player of his time. It had a slight topspin, though he often got a sidespin when hitting down the line. He could hit a placement from any spot on the court. The opponent who attempted to serve and come in on Don generally lost the point outright."

And his serve? "He fired his share of aces, though not as many as Ellsworth Vines or Barry MacKay, but he had a lot of confidence in it, particularly in his younger days."

According to Moffet, Budge was always in top physical shape. As an amateur he never tired. He had big lungs and was seldom short of breath. The only time Jim saw him physically not in form was when he won the French title during his grand slam. A stomach disorder had left Budge so weak he had to eat a sandwich in the middle of the match.

Budge was great in doubles competition. When teamed up

with Gene Mako, his inseparable companion, Gene was the playmaker, but Budge's backhand, volley, and serve won for them. For three years the pair were all but invincible. One of the more memorable doubles matchups of all time was against the Aussie pair, Bromwich and Quist.

Don also played mixed doubles with Alice Marble, and they were great together.

The Helen Wills—
Helen Jacobs Feud

HELEN WILLS DOMINATED tennis in her time as no woman has since Suzanne Lenglen. I first knew her in the mid-1920s. Because of her success at Wimbledon, London newspapers hung onto every word she uttered (and some she didn't). I got more than one exclusive from Helen merely by phoning her at her Berkeley home. She was always cooperative.

We became good friends at a fight in the old San Francisco Armory between Mickey Walker and Cowboy Jack Willis. Wills was there because she was doing black-and-white sketches of athletes in action for United Features. We sat together at ringside.

In the opinion of an overwhelming number of experts, Wills, "Little Miss Poker Face," was the outstanding competitor of her time on the courts. But to tell her story really requires talking about two Helens—Wills and Jacobs. Jack Dempsey and Gene Tunney got along like a couple of wounded hippos in their time, but later they patched up their differences and became good friends.

Not so Wills and Jacobs. Their feud smoldered through all their competitive years and continued after both had hung up their racquets.

It all started with an afternoon in San Francisco when Jacobs, a teenager, got excused from school to go over to Berkeley and practice with Wills. Pop Fuller, her coach at Golden

167

Gate Park, wanted Jacobs to test her ability against a proven player. Fuller at times coached both Wills and Jacobs.

"I dressed for this game with infinite care," Jacobs told me, "for I felt appearances on a court counted for a lot. Miss Wills looked very efficient in her white visor as we started to rally. I realized for the first time what speed of shot meant. The ball came from her right hand straight as a die and fast as a bullet."

The match lasted about twenty minutes. Wills won 6-0, 6-0. Her coldness puzzled Jacobs, who was accustomed to more informality on the courts. "At fifteen one can be impressionable," said Jacobs, whose father was an accountant on my paper, the *Call Bulletin*.

"I wondered if the changing expression on Wills's face and her silence when we passed at the net was deep concentration—or was it a psychological weapon? I hadn't played my best, but she didn't give me a chance to do so."

Jacobs thought Wills had built a formidable game around physical strength. Wills's reflexes were lightning-quick and she had unorthodox footwork. She fought on a court like Tunney in a ring, with implacable concentration and undeniable skill, but without the imagination of a Suzanne Lenglen.

On one occasion Jacobs told me, "There's no doubt but that aloofness crushed many of her less experienced opponents. To play Wills was to play a machine. There was no conversation, no volatility. Our matches became less and less agreeable."

Their animosity—perhaps incompatibility is a better word—was heightened in the spring of 1929 when the U.S. Lawn Tennis Association announced a team would be sent to Europe for a series of international matches. It would consist of Wills and a partner of her choosing.

"That year I ranked second only to Wills among women players," Jacobs reminded me. "I expected to be invited. Instead, she chose Edith Cross."

In their first U.S. championship matches, Wills defeated Jacobs 6-2, 6-1. Newspaper accounts said Jacobs cried afterward, but she denied it to me. "I don't think women are any more given to tears than men, nor is their enthusiasm any more intense," she argued.

Their second and most memorable meeting was in the summer of 1933 when they again came together in the U.S. finals. "I had determined," Jacobs said, "to go to the net at every opportunity. There was no point in standing in the backcourt swapping drives with one so devastating. I put everything I had into the force and placement of my service with the intention of drawing her out of court for the drive to the opposite side, then going to the net."

Jacobs won a hard-fought first set 8-6, but realized she had to maintain her game at the same level for two more sets if necessary, hoping fatigue would impair Wills's coordination and timing. "She lashed out with blistering drives, and with desperate risk I went to the net on anything close to her back line. She won that second set 6-3."

In the deciding one, with a 3-0 lead, Jacobs turned to the ball boy for the balls, to begin her serve. When she faced front again, Wills had walked to the umpire's stand and was reaching for her sweater. It was a confusing moment for Jacobs, who went to her opponent as she was putting on her sweater.

Jacobs asked if she wouldn't like to rest awhile.

"No," was Wills's response. "I can't go on."

As Jacobs was putting on her own street clothes, Elizabeth Ryan came into the locker room in a state of wild excitement. Wills, her partner in the doubles, had announced she would play in the doubles finals just about to start. The officials, however, would not permit this after she had just defaulted in the singles.

"I couldn't dispute her statement that she was on the verge

of fainting when she defaulted, but the fact that she walked back to her Forest Hills apartment and wanted to play in the doubles really embarrassed me."

The last time the two Helens met on the court was in the Wightman Cup finals in England during the blistering summer heat of 1938. In the quarterfinals, Jacobs injured a tendon on her right heel. In the semifinals, Alice Marble gave her a long, hard set that aggravated the injury.

Then in the first set with Wills, the score was tied at 4-all when Wills started peppering Jacobs with short, crosscourt returns. Attempting to reach one return, Jacobs made a leap and landed on her injured foot with a jar. But she wouldn't quit. "I couldn't run for anything," Jacobs said. From that moment on, it was just a breeze for Wills, who won easily.

Wightman came out on the court to urge Jacobs to stop, fearing permanent injury if she went on. The Wightman referred to is Hazel Wightman, for whom the Wightman Cup is named. I often interviewed her when she came out to visit her native Berkeley on the San Francisco Bay from her Boston home.

Wightman began playing tennis when she was fifteen. At that time (prior to World War I), tennis, along with croquet, was considered about the only ladylike game. In 1902 there were only two tennis courts in Berkeley. One was on the University of California campus; the other at the Faculty Club. Talk about the Equal Rights Amendment—women were finally permitted to use these courts from daybreak until eight in the morning, at which time they became exclusive property of males!

"Helen Wills ushered in the mannish power game," Hazel told me, "and while a girl today doesn't have to be an Amazon, she has to have power in her strokes like Little Miss Poker Face or she is left behind." Wills was ruthless on the court, oblivious to all around her. She thought she had to be, to win.

The feud of the two Helens was perhaps the most bitter in

the annals of female sports. Recently I asked Jacobs if she had seen or talked with Wills later on.

"No," she replied, "the last time I saw her was in 1938, in London at the Wimbledon dinner following the tournament." That was over forty-five years ago, so it looks as if they'll never get together.

In a book she wrote called *The Gallery of Champions*, Jacobs ranked the top women players of her time as Lenglen, Wills, Marble, Little, Mallory, Betz, Mathieu, Aussem, Palfrey, Ellis, Brough, Osborne, and Nuthall, in that order.

"Lenglen had everything except a powerful serve," she said. "Wills's backcourt game was her biggest asset."

Alice Marble, who came along after Wills to become a Wimbledon champion, agreed partially. She recently told me, "France's Suzanne Lenglen was the greatest woman tennis player ever. She was considered the female genius of the courts. When she and Mary K. Browne played in their pro tour of 1926 I was thirteen and my brother Dan took me to see her play.

"As for American women, Wills had the greatest record."

Bob Mathias, Schoolboy Hero

DURING THE 1948 London Olympics when it became apparent Bob Mathias, then a high school boy of seventeen, was about to win the decathlon for the United States, I put in a call to his hometown coach, Virgil Jackson, in Tulare. I was sure I could quiz some readable quotes that would shed light on this young phenom, all but completely unknown internationally (even nationally).

Bob was almost a stranger to the sports page at the time. I for one had scarcely heard of him. Jackson gave me a graphic account of how Bob had overcome the tremendous obstacle of childhood anemia to emerge robust enough to compete successfully in track and field's most grueling event.

Even more amazing was Jackson's revelation that both he and Bob had learned about some of the ten decathlon events by reading up on them in elementary instruction books. And he told how other coaches had helped out. Jackson was only forty at the time. "I'm sort of a jack-of-all-trades, but master of none," he told me.

As in high schools of many towns the size of little Tulare, Jackson was primarily a football coach, doubling up in the spring in track and field. What little he learned about track was absorbed from old Carl Schladerman at Washington State. "My own accomplishments were nil," Jackson said. "I put the shot a little and threw the discus, and I wasn't much good at either. In fact, I made my letter only as a freshman. The other three years I couldn't even make the varsity squad.

"About all I could teach Mathias were the rudiments of the shot put and discus. But the basketball coach at Tulare High here was a hurdler of sorts at Chico State and he helped me with Bob. It was in the spring of 1947 that I sensed the tremendous potential he had for the decathlon. This was right after the West Coast Relays.

"Bob did so well in every event he tried I told him he should go in the decathlon, but I never dreamed he'd make it in time for the Olympics the following year.

"In fact, I told him that if he'd start training right away, he might qualify for the Helsinki Olympics in 1952. I pointed out to him that he'd be a senior in college (at Stanford) by that time and would have the benefit of being more mature physically—and also better coaching would be available for such a specialized event."

Jackson said Bob didn't even know exactly what events comprised the decathlon at the time. "And I wasn't dead sure about all of them myself!"

Bob wasn't interested at first. "He was a modest boy, and to give him confidence I told him he was the best all-around athlete I'd ever seen or even heard of, including the great Jim Thorpe."

So the coach and pupil began to bone up on all the decathlon events. They studied books and learned all about the meter and the centimeter. The amazing thing is that up until just a month or so before the games in London, Mathias had never even competed in six of the ten events that comprise the sport.

He had never had a bamboo pole (then used for the pole vault) in his hands until the interscholastic meet in Pasadena eight weeks before the Olympics. It was at this meet that he competed for the first time in the long (then called broad) jump, javelin, one hundred–, four hundred–, and fifteen hundred–meter runs.

"He just picked up the javelin and heaved it," Jackson related. "There was nothing I knew about it that I could teach him. But he had become a pretty good discus thrower prior to the Pasadena meet. And he showed aptitude as a hurdler, though he was very green at it. Funny thing—he didn't even qualify for the hurdles in the California state prep divisional meet. He lost a shoe at the start and finished with only one of them on. Yet he still ran fourth.

"If conditions had been right, Bob, for all his inexperience in the pole vault, might have taken first place in that event in London. He got only 11 feet, 5 3/4 inches in the finals there, but I saw him do 12 feet, 6 inches on our little field here in Tulare. This would have easily won him a first in London."

At that time I asked the coach what made Bob tick as an athlete, for I had never even heard of him until his name cropped up over the sports wires. Jackson listed his attributes first as his natural ability; second, his response to the call of competition; and third, his manner of living.

"But, truth to tell," Jackson went on, "Bob was a much better football prospect than track and field man. He was my fullback and made more yardage than the ball carriers of all our opponents combined. His average per carry from scrimmage was 8.2 yards and he averaged 31 yards on punt and kickoff returns. He completed over half his passes. On defense (they went both ways then) he was a demon. In fact, his defensive play often outshone his ball carrying. And he averaged fifty minutes play per game."

Later, Jackson was to witness the celebration in Tulare the day Bob won in the London decathlon finals. There was singing and dancing in the streets. "That same day," he said, "mothers and fathers kept calling me at my home to ask where they could purchase discus, vaulting poles, and other track and field equipment for their sons."

Pop Warner on Nevers and Thorpe

GLENN SCOBEY WARNER, better known to millions of football fans as just Pop, invented and innovated the famous wingback system that dominated the football game for decades prior to the advent of T formation. He coached Stanford for years where his protégé was Ernie Nevers. He had also coached Jim Thorpe at Carlisle Institute. Pop always maintained that these were the two greatest fullbacks he ever coached. Once, when he was quoted as picking Thorpe as his number one back, Pop denied it. "Both were brilliant," he said, careful never to praise one over the other.

Pop dearly loved to chide T-formation addicts and strike a grumpy pose in talking about the "man in motion" and the other "newfangled doodads" of the game, but beneath this brusque exterior he was conscious of the complex problems of high-geared modern football and was very tolerant of its coaches.

He was chock-full of good football yarns and anecdotes drawn from his personal experiences. One of his favorites was about the first football game he ever played in his life. This was shortly after enrolling at Cornell. Out of curiosity he watched the team's opening practice. The coach saw him standing around and said, "Warner, I've got an extra jersey. Why don't you try out?"

"Don't mind if I do," Pop replied.

Two weeks later, he played all sixty minutes of the opener against Syracuse. After the final gun barked, the man who competed against him on the other side of the line congratulated him on his fine play. Pop was astonished. "This is the first game I ever played," he apologized.

"Mine, too," confessed his Syracuse opponent.

In an interview with me a few years before I was a pall-bearer at his funeral after his death at eighty-three in Palo Alto, Pop twitted Cal Coach Pappy Waldorf for having a staff of eight assistants.

"In my early days as a head coach," Pop said, "we had only two part-time coaches. One was an undertaker. Days he had a funeral he didn't show up, and I took charge of the squad alone. My other part-time assistant was a doctor who laid off every time he had to deliver a baby."

Pop delighted in telling of his Carlisle experiences, and was particularly sentimental when it came to his star there, Jim Thorpe. In the late 1930s Warner was invited to attend the preview in San Francisco of the film, *Jim Thorpe, All-American*, which depicted the tragic story of the great athlete's life. At the end of the showing Pop was asked to give his impressions of the film. He got to his feet slowly and tried to speak, but the words wouldn't come. He dried tears with his handkerchief and, with difficulty, said sobbingly, "I'm terribly sorry, but I am unable to speak at this time."

The next day when he had recovered his composure, I asked him what he thought of the film. "It was a fine, accurate narrative," he said. "And I thought Charles Bickford (who played Warner) was more true to life than I was. And handsomer, too."

At Carlisle, Pop tripled in brass as football, baseball, and track coach, not to mention lacrosse. He loved to tell of a track meet with Lafayette during the Thorpe days. The Lafayette coach phoned him and, explaining that the coming Saturday was homecoming day for the school and no sports event was scheduled, asked if Carlisle would like to come over and engage in a dual meet.

"We'll be there," said Pop.

The "squad" took the interurban train to Lafayette and the Lafayette coach met Pop at the station. "Where is your squad?" he asked.

"This is it," replied Pop, pointing to four Indians—Thorpe, Guyon, Mount Pleasant, and Sweetcorn. The disappointed Lafayette coach suggested calling the meet off. But Pop said he'd guarantee the four-man squad could give a good account of itself.

Thorpe alone won six firsts, some in events in which he had never before competed. Guyon, Mount Pleasant, and Sweetcorn won all the other firsts except the pole vault. None of the Carlisles had ever competed in this difficult event, so Pop conceded the points by default.

Sweetcorn was a favorite of Pop's at Carlisle—a young man fresh off an Oklahoma reservation, who had never slept in anything but a tepee. Conducting his first routine Saturday night bed check, Warner opened Sweetcorn's room and found the bed still made, the cover undisturbed. Concluding that the young Indian must have been out on the town, Pop started to leave the room, when suddenly he heard a loud snore from under the bed. Warner roused Sweetcorn and asked why he didn't want the comfort of the bed instead of sleeping under it.

"What if it rains?" asked Sweetcorn.

When Pop's ace, Ernie Nevers, had two broken ankles confronting a classic Rose Bowler with Notre Dame, the casts were still on. Bone specialists were unable to fashion braces according to Warner's specifications so he fixed them himself, taping rubber inner tubes to Ernie's heels and fastening them to the backs of his knees to serve as artificial tendons.

Nevers played, carried the ball thirty-seven times that day against the Fighting Irish, starring with brilliantly whirling spinners and double reverses.

Never Another Nevers

COLLEGE FOOTBALL RARELY saw the likes of Ernie Nevers. Though not a native son, Ernie found fame at Stanford and went on to make an indelible mark in pro. What other athlete ever had the unique distinction of competing against Ty Cobb, Babe Ruth, Lou Gehrig, and Tris Speaker in baseball and Red Grange, Jim Thorpe, and Bronko Nagurski in football?

Ernie's number 1 jersey was the only one ever retired at Stanford. Nevers was a star in every sport he tried. Stanford's greatest all-time fullback, he was a product of the purple prose era known as the Golden Age of Sports. He was on everybody's All-American team in 1924 and 1925; Pop Warner, his coach, called him the greatest all-around athlete he had ever had, not excluding another of his protégés, Jim Thorpe of the Carlisle Indians.

Although Ernie's feats on the gridirons are best known, he was also an outstanding power hitter and right-hand pitcher, a star forward in basketball, and might have been a great track-and-field man had college baseball not occupied his time in the spring.

One of the better-known Nevers epics was when Stanford met California in a baseball game and dual track meet the same day. In the sixth inning Nevers ran over to the track in his ball uniform, hurled the javelin, and threw the discus, scoring enough points to win the meet. Then he hurried back to the baseball field to complete a shutout and hit a ninth-inning homer. This was Frank Merriwell stuff.

But for old football injuries, Nevers might have become a good major-league pitcher. He played several seasons for the St. Louis Browns under Manager Dan Howley. Two of the homers Babe Ruth hit in 1927 when he bashed sixty were off Nevers at old Sportsman's Park in St. Louis.

They were the Bambino's eighth of the season (in May) and forty-first (in August). Ernie vividly recalled that first one off him. "It started off like a low line drive over the mound," he said, "and I ducked. The ball sailed just over my head and kept rising until it left the park. I was told a low sinking pitch to the outside corner was Ruth's weakness, and that is just what I threw him. But I did strike him out a couple of times."

Nevers was born in Willow River, Minnesota, June 11, 1903. He played some prep football in Superior, Wisconsin, then moved with his parents to California, where he enrolled at Santa Rosa High. On the same squad was Joe Dearing, outdoors editor of the old San Francisco *Call Bulletin* when I was sports editor. I once asked Nevers, "Just how good was Dearing?"

"Only our squad's MVP is all," he replied.

"But how could he be that with you on the team?" I asked.

"He did all my algebra for three years hard running to keep me from flunking out," explained Ernie.

Nevers's Stanford teammates nicknamed the big blond "Big Dog." He was truly a dream athlete and off the field he reminded me of a big, friendly, docile Newfoundland. In many respects he was the perfect football player. He had power, was a great line plunger, was very fast after his first few strides, was fast enough to be called a great open-field runner, and was an excellent passer and kicker. Dan Liebendorfer, Stanford sports publicist for forty years, called him the best linebacker he had ever seen.

Ernie wasn't one of those underpaid pros of his time. He first signed for just one game, a postseasoner in Jacksonville, Florida, for which he got twenty-five thousand dollars, cash on the barrel head, leading a team against Red Grange's AllStars. In those days twenty-five thousand dollars was a lifetime fortune. The game promoter ran away with most of the money, but Ernie had already received—and counted—his money.

When he turned pro, Stanford old grads didn't like it at all. Playing pro in those days was, to them, about as elevating as being a bootlegger. "I needed the money," Nevers once explained to me. "I had debts at Stanford and—this sounds corny, but I needed to lift the mortgage on my dad's Sonoma ranch."

All the pros were after Ernie. He signed two contracts—one with the baseball Browns, the other with the football Duluth Eskimos, then members of the twenty-club National Football League.

Pro footballers had to be iron men in Ernie's time. Except for big stars like him, they were hired for just one game—a game at a time. And one hundred dollars per contest was considered good money. Players could be hired and fired at will. Nearly all of them played all sixty minutes, both ways. And they had to lug their shoulder pads and other heavy equipment around with them in a duffel bag from city to city. The bus was the chief mode of transportation. The legal squad limit was twenty-two, but the Eskimos could only afford to carry sixteen men.

The wear and tear on Ernie was considerable. Once he played with an appendix on the verge of rupturing. He began making records from the start. The first year, standing on his own forty-yard line, he heaved the blunt-nosed pigskin a record-smashing fifty-four yards to Joe Rooney for a touchdown.

The next year he hung up a new pro record by tossing seventeen passes against Pottstown and completing them all. In one game he kicked five field goals in as many attempts.

Some of his records still stand. The one he is most proud of occurred on an icy field in Chicago, 1929, when he led the then Chicago Cardinals to a stunning 40-6 upset of the Chicago Bears, defending champions—perhaps the most humiliating defeat ever suffered by George Halas.

In this game Ernie scored all forty points—six touchdowns and four extra points. Years later Halas told me, "Nevers and Bronko Nagurski were the two best fullbacks I ever saw. Both didn't need interference. They could run their own."

"I don't know how much yardage I gained that day," Ernie told me. "They didn't keep complete statistics those days."

Ernie was among the very first to be selected for the NFL's Football Hall of Fame in Canton, Ohio. He went in along with Grange, Nagurski, Thorpe, Sammy Baugh, Mel Hein, Johnny Blood McNally, Cal Hubbard, and Fats Henry.

Regarding those selections by the committee of which I was a member, Ernie said, "I'm glad you didn't overlook a couple of linemen. Hubbard played for the Packers when I was with the old Chicago Cardinals. He was one of the greatest. Fats Henry played for Pottsville when I was an Eskimo. He was a hell of a lot easier to run around than through."

Red Grange,
"the Galloping Ghost"

As a FLEDGLING sportswriter on the old San Francisco *Call Bulletin* I was assigned to escort Red Grange, "the Galloping Ghost," to meet that newspaper's carrier boys. This was several months after Grange turned pro. That weekend he played in one of the first pioneer pro football games ever played on the West Coast. In spite of the big buildup, the game drew a small crowd at Ewing Field, out in the Fog Belt.

I didn't see him again to talk to until the late 1950s, when the famed redhead came to Kezar Stadium to broadcast a game for his old boss, George Halas of the Chicago Bears. Recalling his initial appearance in San Francisco, Red mentioned, "I never dreamed this city would turn out to be the great pro football town it has. There were only two men back in the mid-1920s who could see it. They were George Halas and Curley Lambeau—Halas in particular.

"George never doubted but that some day the then-scrubby pro game would reach the heights. The Bears kept losing money. Halas put all his profits from real estate and his laundry into his football team, and it almost broke him. But he always told me some day it would run into millions of dollars, and anything he has made is surely coming to him."

Getting back to his San Francisco appearance in the 1920s, Grange mentioned, "I guess I was the only person in the old National Football League ever to play on a percentage basis. I signed with the Bears on Thanksgiving Day, and that winter we played twenty-seven games around the country. In one stretch I played eight games in fourteen days, going both ways, on offense and defense. The promoters wanted to cash in on my college rep at Illinois while it was still fresh in the fans' minds. We drew very well about everywhere but San Francisco. In New York, seventy-three thousand turned out for a Polo Grounds battle, Bears vs. Giants, and from then on pro grid was made."

Red didn't mind minting money while the minting was good. That winter he was paid over one hundred thousand dollars, which was like a million today. He and his business manager, C. C. ("Cash and Carry") Pyle, went partners in a two thousand–acre dude ranch up near Cloverdale in the Mendocino country inland from the Northern California coast. They stocked it with saddle horses, expecting a big play, but along came the 1929 depression and they were wiped out. "I'd like to drive up there some day and look the place over," Red sighed. "I never did get to see my land or the horses."

But it didn't make a bitter man of him. Today he is not wealthy by any means, but he lives comfortably with his wife of thirty years, Margaret. And he doesn't claim they don't play football as well as in his day.

Grange was always humble. A boy from the small town of Wheaton, near Chicago, he showed up uninvited for football practice at Illinois. He had come to get an education (he was a good student) and to play basketball and compete in track and field, not football (though he had made seventy-four touchdowns at Wheaton High, which had an enrollment of about 250). But Red's fraternity brothers insisted he go out for football.

So he suited up. The first day they lined up about one hundred freshmen backfield candidates and had them do three fifty-yard sprints. Grange just breezed in all three heats.

His record at Illinois over the next three years was phenomenal. Best remembered was his performance against Michigan in his junior year. Both teams were unbeaten in their fifth game of the season. Red's performance that breezy autumn day was perhaps the greatest individual accomplishment in all of college football annals. He returned Michigan's opening kickoff of ninety-five yards for a touchdown. In the next twelve minutes, he stunned the Wolverines with sixty-seven-, sixty-six-, and forty-four-yard touchdown runs, whereupon Coach Bob Zuppke pulled him for a breather, but then put him back in the third period when he scored again. He threw a final pass for his last score. Red's field day was all the sweeter because Michigan's coach, "Hurry Up" Yost, had popped off that "all Grange can do is run."

In 1951 I went back with the California team for its game with Illinois at Champaign-Urbana. In the game the Illini quarterback was none other than Tom Haller, later San Francisco Giants catcher and general manager.

We sat with Bob Zuppke before the game. "You know," said Zup, "Red never had a bad day with us and never a greater one than in that Michigan game.

"He had speed, of course, but also a change of pace, rare slipperiness, and a ramrod-straight arm. Red came on our campus from a motherless home in Wheaton. Yost said all he could do was run, and that was like saying all Paderewski could do was play the piano. But Red could pass and block and he was also a fine punter, but I didn't use him at it because we had a great kicker in Earl Britton.

"But Red was the greatest open-field runner ever. He had absolutely no lost motion. He didn't appear to be running fast until you saw somebody trying to catch him and losing ground with every stride. He was never off balance and I never saw a runner better at using his blockers. On a wide play, no matter where his blockers were, he'd pick up a teammate and use him, then employ a sharp cut or an S turn to get in the clear.

"He had a long stride that changed with his pacer. He ran

184

with his knees high. All a tackler could get, usually, was a piece of him.

"He was the soul of graciousness, giving his blockers credit for his long touchdown runs. He was modest, quiet, and sort of a loner. Didn't hang around much with the team. After that great game against Michigan, he put on a sweater and an old cap and went to a movie in town with his roommate."

Red had come to Illinois as an unsung prepster. Zup always had a huge squad and he placed Red on the seventh team for openers.

What made Grange so great? Red himself couldn't tell you, though he said his main asset was his speed. "And that you can't coach. I have always said anything I had going for me in football was that I could run." And of course the source of his speed was his powerful legs.

In his day there were no such things as scholarships for athletes. (Zup told me Grange came to the campus with only one suit and an extra pair of pants, a sweater, and a toothbrush.) He received no money, no nothing. And there were no soft jobs during the school year. To get to the university and stay there necessitated a full-time summer job. He said he was lucky to strike up a friendship with a man who had an ice route in Wheaton. During three years in high school and summer vacations in college, he delivered two hundred–pound chunks of ice. The ice-wagon job did far more than benefit him financially.

"I'd walk along beside the wagon all day long, was never off my legs, and that did more to develop me as a football player than anything I know of. I'd get up at five in the morning and probably make sixty or seventy stops a day, walking up and down stairs and walking mile after mile. Nobody would work that hard just exercising. I still say working on that ice wagon six days a week did me more good than anything I've ever done in my life."

Grange played his last game of football in Los Angeles against the old New York Giants. He knew it was time to quit, he said, when he slipped through a big hole in the line and was headed for a touchdown when the slowest lineman on the opposing team caught him from behind.

He signed a lucrative movie contract, starring in the film *One Minute to Go*. Later he did the color or the play-by-play for Chicago Bears, bowl, or all-star games. A heart murmur twenty years ago caused him to give up broadcasting, and since then he has lived a quiet life in Florida, seldom venturing out even for games in nearby Tampa. Grange is definitely not a bitter recluse. His red thatch has turned to a dull rust, but he is still ruggedly handsome and always has a smile for visiting friends from his days as a superstar.

Present at the Creation:
The First NFL Hall of Fame

THE BOARD OF selectors for the Pro Football Hall of Fame faced a formidable challenge at their first meeting in 1963 at the Waldorf Astoria in New York City. How many charter enshrinees would be chosen, and from which years? What criteria would be used for the candidates from the early period, when there were no elaborate offensive statistics and sacks were for potatoes instead of defensive players?

Unlike today's twenty-nine-member group (one media representative from each NFL city, plus the president of the Pro Football Writers Association), the initial board consisted of fourteen men: Lewis Atchison, *Washington Star*; Arthur Daley, *New York Times*; Art Daley, *Green Bay Press*; Chuck Heaton, *Cleveland Plain Dealer*; Herb Good, *Philadelphia Inquirer*; Sam Greene, *Detroit News*; Charlie Johnson, *Minneapolis Star*; Paul Menton, *Baltimore Evening Sun*; Bob Oates, *Los Angeles Examiner*; George Strickler, *Chicago Tribune*; Jack Sell, *Pittsburgh Post-Gazette*; and myself from the San Francisco *Call Bulletin*. There were two others who weren't active sportswriters: Davey O'Brien, a Fort Worth radio-TV announcer who used to play quarterback for the Philadelphia Eagles; and Jimmy Conzelman of St. Louis, who had played on four pro clubs in the 1920s and had coached two world championship teams, the Chicago Cardinals (1947) and Providence Steamrollers (1928).

The board selected players from two periods. The first began in 1892 when Pudge Heffelfinger became the first known professional. The other era started in 1920 with the birth of the first organized pro football league—the American Professional Football Association—in Canton, Ohio, the home of the Hall of Fame. There were twenty-two clubs in that first league, which officially became known as the National Football League (NFL) in 1922, and a franchise could be purchased for fifty dollars.

The committee generally agreed that Jim Thorpe, Red Grange, and Ernie Nevers rated charter enshrinement, but there wasn't complete accord at first. An enshrinee today needs approximately 80 percent approval of the voters. An inductee had to be chosen unanimously at that first session.

One writer felt that Nevers didn't deserve to be inducted with the first group. He changed his mind after a phone call to George Halas, who reminded the dissenter that Nevers was a one-man football team for the Chicago Cardinals when he scored all of his team's forty points in an upset of Halas's Bears in 1929.

Even Grange came under close scrutiny because his professional achievements paled in comparison to his college record. Injuries limited Grange's longevity as a pro at times and confined him mainly to defense. But Grange's contributions to the game couldn't be measured by statistics.

The committee also agreed that the Hall of Fame shouldn't be reserved only for players, but also should include those who had made outstanding contributions to the game. There had been arguments over admitting coaches and owners in the charter group, but nobody could deny acceptance of Halas, the founder-owner-coach of the Bears. He attended the NFL organizational meeting in the showroom of a Canton Hupmobile garage in 1920, and was the only person associated with the league throughout its first fifty years, serving as a coach for forty years.

Halas's selection cleared the way for others, such as Earl

("Curly") Lambeau, founder, coach, and general manager of the Green Bay Packers; and Bert Bell, the NFL commissioner from 1946 to 1959 who led the league to unprecedented heights by setting up farsighted television policies and recognizing the NFL Players Association. Club owners George Preston Marshall (Redskins) and Tim Mara (Giants) were also voted in, along with Joe Carr, a former sportswriter who had served as NFL president from 1921 to 1930.

Halas and Conzelman were particularly helpful in supplying vital information and judgment on the first linemen picked for the Hall of Fame, because all the committee members had to work from were one-paragraph profiles and a few newspaper clippings on the leading candidates. The first lineman approved, Wilbur ("Pete") Henry, was a 250-pound tackle who played for three teams in the 1920s and held the record for the longest punt (ninety-four yards). Bronko Nagurski was one of the most enthusiastically accepted. Three others—Sammy Baugh, Don Hutson, and Earl ("Dutch") Clark—were unanimous choices.

Today the minimum number of players inducted in one year is three, the maximum six. The first selection committee voted in seventeen, the largest class ever: Jim Thorpe, Red Grange, Ernie Nevers, Sammy Baugh, Bronko Nagurski, Bert Bell, Joe Carr, Dutch Clark, Mel Hein, Pete Henry, Cal Hubbard, Don Hutson, George Halas, Curly Lambeau, George Preston Marshall, Johnny Blood McNally, and Tim Mara.

Even though there was some disagreement over players' selection, time has proven that the NFL would not be what it is today without them!

49er Unforgettables

To WRITE OF the old-time 49ers, I mean mostly the original cast of players who came along in 1946, is like trying to paint a landscape on a postage stamp. Their deeds were memorable. This will be no chronological passing review—only a depiction of some dramatic moments as they come to mind. The original backfield was Frankie Albert at quarterback, Norm Standlee at full, Len Eshmont at left half, and Johnny "Strike" Stryzkalski at right half.

Two of them hung up their moleskins on the same December day at Kezar Stadium six years later. One of the real heartthrobbers was that final game of Strike and Frankie. They had thrilled Bay Area fans for years, Frankie during the Wow Boy Era at Stanford and Stryzkalski playing service team football.

Earlier in the week the two had announced that next Sunday's game would be their last. Both had launched their pro careers in the old All-America Conference with a win over the Los Angeles Dons seven seasons before. The other two, Eshmont and Standlee, had already bowed out.

And now, when the squad charged on the field, the 49er band struck up, appropriately enough, "Frankie and Johnny." Albert had a great afternoon quarterbacking his team to a 24-14 win over the Green Bay Packers. There were some improvisations in the script for Frankie's bow out. Several minutes were left on the clock when the 49ers' defensive platoon went in and Frankie shuffled back to the bench. He concluded that the game was over for him.

Off came one shoe, He flung it to a crowd of small boys in back of the bench. Off came the other, then his socks, shoulder pads, the revered Albertonian helmet, and the tattered number 13 jersey—all of which were flung to the kids.

The script had called for him to be sent in for one play as soon as the 49ers regained possession of the ball. After that one final thrust he was to have been dramatically yanked by Coach Buck Shaw to make a grand exit from the field of play. But when Buck ran an eye down the bench he saw Albert standing like a plucked chicken, with only his pants on. So, a few seconds before the final gun, Frankie made for the Kezar tunnel en route to the dressing room in advance of his mates. A misty-eyed group of sentimental fans had congregated above and around the tunnel exit. Albert, perhaps the most genuine realist in the crowd, jogged out of the stadium like an exultant schoolboy on the last day of June classes.

Seconds later the whole squad filed into the clubhouse and Frankie was handed the game ball. This was his farewell to sports, he must have thought, though he was later to play in Canada and come back as head coach for the 49ers.

I asked Frankie after the game what his greatest moment on the field had been, lifetime. He said as a pro it was the 48-20 thumping of the Cleveland Browns in 1949 that he'd remember the longest. As a Joe Colleger at Stanford, he said it was when Stanford was rolling toward the Rose Bowl in 1940 with only the USC Trojans blocking the way. The score was tied 7-7 when he heaved a long pass to Fred Meyer to set up a winning marker.

There were some lows, too. He thought the lowest was in the 1941 Cal game at Berkeley. Nobody had ever blocked a kick on him until that day, when Bob Reinhardt, Bears tackle, busted through. "I thought there was something I was doing wrong when he blocked another. So I had Al Cole punt the next time and they blocked his kick, too."

During the four years the 49ers were in the old AAFC, Strike gained 2,451 yards for a 5.4 per-carry average at right half. Only Marion Motley, Browns fullback, topped him as the all-time ground gainer of the old days. A few days before Johnny retired I kidded him, stating I had spent nearly seven years trying to spell his name right in the paper, and just when I had mastered it, he up and quit.

Fans had seen very little of Johnny his final season. Mostly he just sat around. He played only eleven minutes all year. About the only time they sent Johnny in was when the 49ers kicked off. A deadly tackler, he would head straight into a wedge and, with reckless abandon, break it up.

This partially accounted for the fact that he had his nose broken six times in his seven years as a 49er. In fact, the first thing he and Albert did after bowing out was report to the San Francisco hospital on Monday to get plastic nose and face lifts.

Strike's unforgettable deeds with the 49ers in happier seasons have lived long in the memory of fans and will be passed along for generations to come. He will be remembered as perhaps the finest "clutch" player of them all in the formulative years of the club.

In his prime, Johnny was a sixty-minute man. Offense or defense, it was all the same to him. He gave all he had every minute. His most unforgettable play in my memory was a crucial run he made against the 49ers' most hated rival, the pesky Cleveland Browns. It was in 1948, at Kezar. Johnny took a pitchout from Albert and went around right end. Three times he was knocked flat on his kisser by Brownies tacklers bigger than he. Each time, he got up (as the rules permitted in those days). He was finally brought down, but not until he had gone thirty yards and set up the winning touchdown in a game that saw the 49ers triumph 30-28.

Anyone who watched that play will never forget it. More than any other, it typified his style and indomitable spirit. And before he broke an ankle in 1949, Johnny was the one always called on to carry the ball when yardage had to be made. Any veteran on those early day squads will tell you this.

"He was our most competitive player through the years," was the tribute Albert paid Strike after their final game. "Calling on him to carry in a clutch gave me a rep as a smart quarterback. There was only one thing to do when you just had to have yardage—call Johnny's number. He rarely let the team down. I guess he must have made as many first downs those first four 49er years as anybody in football.

"That pitchout to Johnny was the best play in our bag until he broke his ankle. All he needed was one block and he was gone. Once he circled right end there was no stopping him."

Hugh McElhenny inherited this pitchout play, but not even the great Hurricane executed it in a more devastating manner. Hugh was a fancier, more elusive runner, but Strike was the barroom type. He'd rough and tumble and bull his way right over a bigger man, leaving him flat on the ground.

Stryzkalski came to the 49ers with a unique background, for he had only a freshman's experience in college ball. He left Marquette to go to war in 1942, before his sophomore year. While assembling the original 49er squad, Shaw and Owner Tony Morabito got a tip on him. He was then playing with the Second Air Force. The two flew to Boise in 1944 to watch him. Stryzkalski had a field day against Whitman College. Shaw buttonholed him right after the game and walked away with his signature to play for the 49ers as soon as the war was over.

There was an unusual stipulation in the contract. Strike insisted that a condition of his signing was that the 49ers also ink his buddy, Joe Vetrano, a half-pint halfback. Shaw agreed, with misgivings on account of Vetrano's size. But Joe the Toe was to earn his salt, kicking 107 successive extra points after touchdown, a pro record at the time.

Once, during a time-out, newspaper photographers on the sidelines complained they hadn't been able to get a good close-up shot of Stryzkalski carrying the ball. "I'll take care of that," said Albert. "I'll pitch out to Johnny so that he'll be headed to his right, straight toward you guys."

And Frankie did just that. The play unfolded just as he had said it would.

Stryzkalski had a big hidden asset: a fine sense of humor that stayed with him through emergencies. I was on a 49er plane one night when it was so rough even the stewardesses got sick. Johnny jumped up and served his teammates their meals. There was thunder and lightning over Nebraska and the athletes were getting jumpy. So Johnny took over the loud-speaker and made wisecracks that had the squad in stitches until the plane rode out the storm.

Shaw put Strike in the lineup the day he bowed out, if for nothing else than out of memory for the best running back in pro ball before he broke an ankle. The spirit and dash he gave the 49ers through the years was to become a part of them. "Without it you're lost in pro ball," Buck explained, "and nobody knows it better than I."

The Indestructible Nomellini

To HIS RIVALS in the NFL it must have seemed that Leo "the Lion" Nomellini was around an awfully long time. And he was, too, for he didn't miss a single game for the San Francisco 49ers from the day they first played in the league in 1950 until after the 1963 seasons fourteen long years later.

All told, Leo played in 174 straight regular-season games. Counting preseason and Pro Bowl appearances, the durable tackle was in 266 contests. He was respected by friend and foe alike as one of the greatest linemen ever, both on defense and offense. It was no surprise that he made the San Francisco Bay Area Sports Hall of Fame recently, getting more votes than even Joe Perry and Y. A. Tittle. Besides his great play, Nomellini possessed a good sense of humor that kept the 49ers (the only team he ever played for as a pro) loose at all times. When Frank Albert was head coach he named Leo team captain, knowing the big tackle's spirited play would prove contagious.

Leo always fancied himself a ball carrier and hounded Albert to give him a shot at playing fullback. He got a taste of handling the pigskin when he realized every lineman's dream against one of the greatest Los Angeles Rams teams (1951, with Bob Waterfield, Norm Van Brocklin, Tom Fears, and Crazy Legs Hirsch). He blocked a punt, chased the ball into the end zone, and fell on it for a touchdown.

Then one day he picked up a Sammy Baugh fumble and staggered twenty yards to score. Leo fancied newspaper accounts of this exploit would go something like this: "Leo Nomellini proved to the football world that he has been miscast in the role of tackle. He was a sight to inflamed orbs as he swivel-hipped his way across the goal, ripping off huge gains.

"Repeatedly he reversed his field to shake off tacklers. He jerked customers out of their seats with his cyclonic breakaway with the speed of an antelope, deftly stiff-arming a tackler here and sidestepping another there. Red Grange in his most brilliant days never showed more deception and speed than the brilliant Nomellini today."

Leo's disgust knew no bounds, however, when he read actual accounts of his short run, and claimed that reporters had jobbed him. They called the run only twenty yards, but he said he ran from midfield to pay dirt and distinctly recalled shaking off "at least six" would-be tacklers. He kept begging the fun-loving and do-anything-for-a-laugh Albert, "let me carry the porkhide."

So in the closing minutes of the season's finale, with the 49ers leading a weak Green Bay Packers team by a big score at Kezar, Albert concocted a play in the huddle with Leo lined up at fullback. The 49ers line deliberately collapsed like a sieve as Albert handed off to Nomellini, who was dumped for a six-yard loss.

The final game stats on Leo as a ball carrier read: "Times carried one, yards gained none, yards lost six." It was the first and last time Nomellini carried the ball.

At six foot three and 265 pounds, Leon had size, speed, agility, aggressiveness, and great dedication. Year after year he'd report to camp in better shape than others ten years younger. He could play offense or defense, sometimes going sixty minutes. He was knocked cold only once on the field, by the then-smallest man in pro football, barrel-legged Buddy Young of the Baltimore Colts, a five-foot-five running back. They collided when Leo tackled him. "I was out like a light for five minutes," recalls Leo. But he was back in the game after a short rest on the bench.

Nomellini boasted he was a "quarterback hater." He was one of the best pass rushers ever in the NFL, yet on offense he was a bulldozing pass blocker and adept at opening holes for Perry, McElhenny, and other ball-carrying teammates.

Born in Italy, he came with his parents when he was two to live on Chicago's tough West Side. He attended Crane Tech High but had to pass up sports to put in a full shift in an iron foundry to help support the family. Right after Pearl Harbor he joined the marines, and was sent to a corps camp at Cherry Point, North Carolina, where his size got him a taste of his first football. Later he saw action at Okinawa and when he was discharged, University of Minnesota Coach Bernie Bierman grabbed him.

In the first college game Nomellini ever saw he was a starter. He made All-America two seasons and was also a shot putter, anchorman on the 440 relay team, and Big Ten heavyweight wrestling champ.

Talk about a Horatio Alger character—Nomellini surely was one. He was immensely popular in San Francisco with its large Italian population. The Lion, late in his 49ers career, made a lot of money wrestling as a pro. In one bout against Lou Thesz of St. Louis, Leo drew the largest pro wrestling gate in San Francisco history—seventy-two thousand dollars at the Cow Palace, shocking sports columnists who had given professional wrestling short shrift.

Nomellini's record closely paralleled that of another Minnesota All-American, Bronko Nagurski. Both were tackles, and both later made a name for themselves as wrestlers. It was as if Leo had patterned his athletic career after Nagurski. Indeed, the Lion's pet dog, a boxer, was named Bronko.

Leo headed a successful macaroni and spaghetti manufacturing firm for a time after retiring from football. He now promotes wrestling in the East Bay.

Leo's record in pro football could consume pages. Among other things, he was the 49ers number one choice in the very first National League draft after they were inducted into that league from the old All-America Football Conference. He turned out to be a superb selection. He became one of the few players ever to be named to an all-NFL team on both offense and defense, winning offensive laurels twice and defensive four times, all in the 1950s.

Unlike many athletes, Leo, like wine, kept improving with age. He was still a good tackle when he retired voluntarily at thirty-nine, after fourteen years of being battered by opponents in every way a tackle can be battered. He had truly earned the tag "indestructible."

Nomellini and Joe Perry were the very first 49ers to be inducted into the Pro Football Hall of Fame in Canton. That was in 1969. Leo played in ten Pro Bowl games. Not a bad record for one born in the shadows of the Leaning Tower of Pisa, one who never played prep football, and doubtless one who never would have become an All-American at Minnesota and an all-time, all-NFL pro tackle if it hadn't been for the war.

The Incomparable Marchetti

GINO MARCHETTI HAS all the credentials for gridiron immortality. He anchored the famous unbeaten 1951 University of San Francisco squad, coached by Joe Kuharich. Later he was an all-NFL defensive tackle for seven years, and in 1972 he was enshrined in the NFL's Hall of Fame the very first year he was eligible.

He surely was no "never was." Indeed, he was an illustrious player, but became more or less a forgotten man in the Bay Area because he dropped completely out of the local picture.

This was because he started a chain of fast-food restaurants in the East known as Gino's Inc. This chain grew to three hundred units and made Gino a millionaire. He now lives in Wayne, Pennsylvania.

Perhaps the greatest honor heaped on him was when he was voted the NFL's all-time best defensive end at the league's fiftieth anniversary. He was tapped for this honor by a special panel of experts in 1969, who said a better pass rusher never drew breath. He put more pressure on passers than any man in the pro annals. But he played it clean. Nobody ever leveled "cheap shot" charges against Gino.

While Gino was an all-around brilliant defensive end, he was best known for his pass rushing. He was a holy terror on third down and obvious passing situations. When opponents double-teamed and sometimes even tripled-teamed him, it only served to make the rest of the Colts rushers the more effective.

He was also adept at stopping a running play. He could recover quickly to close the inside holes and could swing wide to stymie the sweeps. Captain of the Colts defense through much of his career, he was not only highly respected by his teammates but also a tremendous favorite with the rabid fans of Baltimore.

Shrewd little Eddie LeBaron of the College of the Pacific (now University of the Pacific), later one of football's smallest quarterbacks (he weighed only 140 pounds sopping wet) with the Washington Redskins, had a way of staying on the good side of Gino.

"He could have racked me up many times," Eddie confided, "but to keep him from getting riled I'd pat him on the back after a tackle and tell him, 'Nice play, Gino—that's the way to break up a pass.' Next time he'd set me down easy. It kept me from getting killed."

And all this about a guy whose parents, Italian immigrants, objected to Gino's playing football for fear he'd get hurt. "Whatever you do, Gino," counseled his pop, "stay out of other boys' way so they no hurt you." Every quarterback in the NFL in the 1950s and early 1960s must have wished Gino had followed his dad's advice.

From Ellis Island his parents settled in West Virginia, where Gino was born. Then they moved to Antioch, California, a historic old river town near the Sacramento's mouth.

Many coaches say Gino created most of the modern defensive end techniques. He was six foot four and 245, and had the strength and meanness to take the pounding of interior line play, but his major contribution was to add finesse and ruggedness to the prototype of superior defensive play.

He was the wheelhorse of the famed defensive line of the Baltimore Colts of the late 1950s. Great as he was for his clean rushing of passers, he was almost equally adept at breaking up the interference to stop rushing thrusts as well.

Ironically, Gino was not around when the Colts had their greatest moment, that unforgettable 23-17 overtime win over the New York Giants in the 1958 championship game. This was before Super Bowls were even a gleam in Pete Rozelle's eyes.

Many think this game was the greatest pro football battle ever played. In it Gino suffered a badly broken ankle late in the game while making a critical tackle of the Giants' great running back, Frank Gifford. Gino's teammate, three hundred–pound Gene "Big Daddy" Lipscomb, fell on top of him after the tackle.

Marchetti's stop proved a key play, for it ended the Giants' drive and gave the Colts the ball. From here they went on to tie the game in the last seconds of regulation time, and then win in overtime. Gino stayed on the sidelines until the score was tied, but was taken to the dressing room during the overtime.

"The docs were afraid the crowd might trample me if we scored," Gino explained on his return to San Francisco. "I was stretched out on a table when I heard the guys coming in. I could tell then we had won. They were all whooping it up. Right then that ankle stopped hurting."

At first it was thought the injury might end Gino's brilliant career, but as it turned out, all it did was prevent him from setting a then all-time record for Pro Bowl appearances—ten of these classics in an eleven-year stretch.

As a prep, Gino never showed a lot until his senior year at Antioch High. Then, at the age of seventeen, he enlisted in the army and fought in Europe's Battle of the Bulge. After the war, he organized the Antioch Hornets team and, while playing bush ball, attracted a Modesto Junior College scout. After Gino spent a year at Modesto, Joe Kuharich sought him out while building the foundation for a great football powerhouse on the University of San Francisco hilltop.

There Gino developed into the finest tackle on the Coast, winning about every honor in 1951. He was to the USF line the bulwark that Ollie Matson was to the backfield. Fittingly, the two hilltoppers made Canton together in 1972.

Part of the sting of USF's not having been invited to some bowl as a reward for an unbeaten season was soothed for Marchetti when he played for the West in the 1952 Shrine Game at Kezar and was one of the most luminous stars in the contest.

Gino's pro career started discouragingly because of the unique team situation that developed after the New York Yankees took him number two in the 1952 draft. The Yankees franchise was shifted to Dallas, but the hapless Texans folded after one season and Gino's contract was assigned to Baltimore, which was setting up shop again after the original Colts had folded in 1950. The Colts were a rank second division outfit, but Marchetti helped them build into a championship squad while he himself developed into a superstar.

He was always determined to retire before he lost his great effectiveness and he tried to quit after the 1963 season, but the Colts had title hopes again in 1964 and talked him into staying on. Almost two years later, in 1966, he was coaxed into playing again when the Colts were hurting due to injuries in the line. He played only four games that year.

49ers McElhenny,
a Genuine Superstar

THIS CHAPTER COVERS the early career of "Hurricane," or "Hurryin,'" Hugh McElhenny. It starts with the day they really took the wraps off Mac in league play. On this occasion in Chicago against the Bears, October 19, 1952, he was a madman, making a shambles of a defense Clark Shaughnessy, a George Halas assistant, had set up to stop him.

Mac, operating from right half, led a 40-16 massacre of the Bears, setting up four touchdowns and running a punt back 94 yards for a fifth. His devastating runs grossed 103 yards on only twelve carries. This total gain doesn't include the passes he caught, thrown by Y. A. Tittle and Frank Albert, who divided game time at quarterback.

Hugh was on the field for less than half the game, in minutes. Afterward, Bernie Masterson was to call him "a combination of McAfee and Nagurski." And Shaughnessy predicted McElhenny was destined to be one of the great running backs of all time.

Mac had shown flashes of genius before they turned him loose on the Bears. In his first exhibition appearance for the 49ers, he ran the opening kickoff back sixty-two yards. Coach Buck Shaw had debated starting him because Hugh was so fidgety while warming up before the game. There was a reason. He had received a telegram two hours before the game that his wife, the former Peggy Ogston, had just borne him their first child.

Buck also wanted to bring Mac along slowly because at the time, Joe Perry was getting him all the yardage needed on the ground. This is why Hugh saw so little action during the exhibition season. Besides the Rams game, they gave him one other shot at packing the ball. Against the then Chicago Cardinals (in another exhibitioner), Tittle tossed him a wide pitchout and Mac rambled forty-two yards before Ollie Matson, an Olympic sprinter and star of the Cardinals, put on his best burst of speed and finally hauled him down. Exit McElhenny from the game.

After league play started, Hugh went eighty-nine yards from scrum to score on Dallas. John Pettibone, the ex-Notre Damer, knocked him down halfway through his epic dash. But McElhenny got up and went on to score.

Much has been made of the story that Tony Morabito ordered McElhenny to be drafted number one out of the University of Washington on the strength of a phone call from Albert in Honolulu (where Mac had just starred in the Hula Bowl). This surely had a lot to do with the drafting of McElhenny, but Shaw had been aware of the Huskies star's electrifying, driving ball toting for several seasons.

During his three years in Seattle, Mac, who had transferred to Washington from Compton Junior College, compiled a then Pacific Coast Conference record of 2,499 yards gained from scrimmage. And Buck had seen him make the longest punt return in the conference's history at the time—100 yards, against USC.

Buck had perused statistics showing the Mac had had many field days for the Huskies. Against Minnesota he had run fifty-six yards to score from scrimmage on an end run and had also scored a last-minute touchdown against the Gophers after intercepting a pass. It gave Washington a 25-20 upset win. And against Oregon, Mac had kicked nine out of nine extra points, while against Stanford he had run sixty-five yards around right end from scrimmage.

Buck was an eyewitness when the Huskies tied strong UCLA (coached by Red Sanders) 20-20, with McElhenny scoring all the points. But the real convincer was Mac's showing against the powerful Bears of Berkeley, whom Pappy Waldorf had forged into a juggernaut. In that one, Mac scored twenty of the Huskies' twenty-eight points.

"It was after watching him that day that I decided to draft him number one," Buck told me flatly. "I certainly have had no cause to regret it." Yet Shaw came in for considerable criticism when he did so. The experts figured he should have grabbed Ollie Matson or Les Richter ahead of Mac.

Shaw wasn't the perfect diagnoser of McElhenny's ability at that. His first thought was to make a receiving end out of him so Mac could grab pitchouts and skedaddle into the end zone. This wasn't a bad idea, but Hugh was to prove more useful in the backfield.

One factor in McElhenny's success as a breakaway running back was that Joe Perry was having a great season the year Hugh broke in with the 49ers. As the cagy Albert put it to me once, "Perry knows he has to go full speed ahead because Mac is breathing down his neck." At one time that season Hugh had a 10-yards-per-carry average, in contrast to Perry's 4.5. Another reason for Mac's successful first season was a greatly improved offensive line, particularly at tackle, where Nomellini, Toneff (the rookie from Notre Dame), Carpella, and Roy Collins alternated.

Getting back to Mac's great game against the Bears his first NFL year, he was presented with the game ball and at the same time, the squad came up with a nickname for him—"The

King." The players had been calling him "Nine Yard" McElhenny before that, but had decided that nickname was doing him an injustice.

Mac was popular with the 49er players. Wearing his rookie laurels gracefully, he was always among the first on the practice field, realizing he was right in the front rank for consideration as NFL rookie of the year.

The Birth of
the Oakland Raiders

WHAT WERE THE Oakland Raiders like just before and after they
played their first game following a hastily organized franchise
in 1960? I was around, writing sports in San Francisco at the
time, but found it necessary to do some research to get some
of the facts. I found the Raiders saga one of the most exciting
in my forty-two years with the old *Call Bulletin* and later the
Examiner.

The American Football League (AFL) was, of course, a
swaddling infant. The research impressed on me that while
Wayne Valley (one of the original owners) and Al Davis (later)
were key people in the success of the organization, the unsung, little-publicized "creator" of the Raiders was really Chet
Soda, Oakland financier. The 49ers lost $150,000 their first
year in pro football. The Raiders finished $400,000 in the red
in 1960, but their stockholders—who, in addition to Valley and
Soda, included Wayne Osborne, Ed McGah, Arthur Becker,
and Don Blessing—were able to withstand the financial shock.
Their combined assets ran into many millions.

At Kezar in the early fall of 1960, the Raiders drew 12,703
at their debut (count on them not to have shortchanged themselves on the crowd count). By comparison, the 49ers drew
31,000 in their 1946 unveiling.

Believe it or not, the Raiders were, in a sense, the brain-
child of none other than Charley Harney, the contractor who
built Candlestick Park. Harney hated pro football. He was an
ardent USF fan. In fact, he financed the building of an unbeaten

USF team (under Joe Kuharich). Harney always contended it was the pros who chased St. Mary's, Santa Clara, and his hilltop alma mater out of Kezar on Sundays—and in truth, it was.

Yet he planted the Oakland Raiders germ. At a wedding anniversary party he gave he came up with the idea out of the blue when he asked Soda, one of his guests, "Why don't you go after a franchise in that new pro football league those Texans are forming? There's one still left and it is going begging. If I didn't have so many irons in the fire I'd buy it myself."

Soda took it from there. He and his dad had formed a small contracting firm years before and had pyramided their building and real estate business into millions. He was a pillar in horse racing, owning stock in Golden Gate Fields, and later on was to become chairman of the powerful California Horse Race Board.

A few days after Harney planted the idea, Frank Leahy, former Notre Dame coach but at the time manager of Barron Hilton's Los Angeles Chargers (before they moved to San Diego), phoned Chet telling him Hilton felt his Chargers were isolated without another California team in the embryonic AFL. By this time Soda had already talked to seven other two-fisted Oakland businessmen who agreed to join him in his venture. Even Harney made a token investment in it.

Because the Raiders were the eighth and last club to get a franchise, they were virtually left at the post for talent. Eddie Erdelatz, who had been hurriedly signed at a then fabulous twenty-five thousand dollars a year on a two-year pact, had to put a club together practically with stickum. Only eight of his squad of forty had previous pro experience. Other clubs in the league had jumped the gun on the date set by the league for opening practice.

By alert maneuvering, Eddie, aided by Wes Frye, talent scout and long a Cal assistant coach, began picking up players like mad when the NFL clubs started pruning down to the player limit. For a time Erdelatz was said to have had three teams: one going, one coming, and one already there. Some players would join the Raiders early in the week and be gone by Saturday. In the final two weeks there were fifteen newcomers on the squad.

It was impossible to mold such a heterogeneous group into a team quickly. The betting in some quarters was that the Raiders wouldn't win a single game their first season. But Eddie was fortunate in finding a quarterback. He came up with Tom Flores right from taw. Although Paul Larson (ex-Cal) and Bob Webb were favored to become the starter, Flores won out. He was from the University of the Pacific. NFL clubs, including the 49ers, were sky-high on him until he injured a shoulder his senior year. After that, they seemed to lose interest. Erdelatz found Flores a smooth ball handler and fine passer, long or short, and Eddie thought he had two good receiving targets in Gene Probola of Boston University and Charlie Hardy, whom the 49ers once had as a defensive back.

Erdelatz stuck his neck out, predicting Flores might become the best t-formation quarterback in the fledgling league. But as the season wore on, Jack Kemp proved the leading passer, overtaking Frank Tripucka of Denver. Kemp was classed as an NFL castoff because he had kicked around in that league three seasons.

One of the first to report at the initial Raiders camp in Santa Cruz was Jim Otto, destined to become a pro football legend. "I could make some NFL clubs I know," he told me, "but it's more of an honor and distinction to be an original member of a brand-new league. That's why I choose to play with the Oakland Raiders."

"C'mon," said his roomie, "You're not a Joe Colleger now. You've been around Canadian football and the NFL and know better. You're here because, just like me, you know it's easier to make the squad and because it's a good living."

There were big gaps to fill on the late-blooming Raiders. So Commissioner Joe Foss got up what he called an "available list" from which the Raiders could "draft" certain players from each of the other seven clubs.

Erdelatz picked George Blanda, property of Houston, which claimed George had a "no transfer" clause in his contract. So that deal was off. The Raiders had first rights to Abner Haynes, but Dallas signed him regardless of Oakland's legal rights.

In spite of all the handicaps, Erdelatz was able to field a respectable team for the opener with Houston at Kezar Stadium. Although the Raiders lost, they impressed onlookers as a "scrappy" rather than "crappy" team. Erdelatz outsmarted the Oilers by having little Jack Larscheid, a halfback, toss a pass to Tony Teresa.

But there were habitually discouraging crowds. In one game that first season the attendance was only 4,136. Trying to compete with the well-entrenched 49ers, the Raiders moved from Kezar to Candlestick Park, and from there to Youell Field, Oakland, until the big Coliseum was built. Little known is the fact that the club tried desperately to lease California Memorial Stadium, on the University of California campus, but was turned down.

Erdelatz finished the season with a highly respectable 6-8 won-and-lost record, considering all the roadblocks of being the last AFL club to get a franchise (and this only a few months before the season was to start).

But before the next season began, Erdelatz was fired. The action came as a surprise to players and fans.

Volney Peters, a seven-year veteran of the NFL, told me, "Eddie was building a winning team. If they'd just stuck with him, he'd have made it big for everybody, including the stockholders. I've played for some fine coaches—Jeff Cravath, Joe Kuharich, and Buck Shaw of the 49ers. In my book Erdelatz was the best. He knew how to coach and how to treat his players. We played our hearts out for Eddie."

Outspoken in his criticism of the firing was Sammy Baugh, king of the forward passers in his day (or any other day). "Erdelatz was one-two with any coach in the league. His firing was unjustified," he said.

Al Davis hadn't yet appeared on the Raiders scene when Erdelatz left. Davis was to become one of the most brilliant pages in pro football history anywhere. He convinced me years ago he was a genius, and I was the first to hang that tag on him. I never could quite analyze just what type of genius he was, but I was sure he was one.

A short while after leaving the Raiders, Erdelatz discovered he had cancer. He died in his early forties. What a great pair he and Davis would have made had they teamed up together!

A Double Rah-Rah for Double O

IT WASN'T ONLY dyed-in-the-wool old Oakland Raiders buffs who were pleased at the selection of Jim Otto as the first Raider to be enshrined in the hard-to-crash pro football Hall of Fame in Canton, Ohio. Pro football fans in general were tickled that a lowly center with the odd jersey number 00 made it instead of some highly paid passer or ball carrier, as is usually the case.

For 15 years Jim anchored the Raiders' offense, becoming known as one of the most dedicated leaders in pro. Little did he realize, when he reported in 1959 for the very first Raider practice session at the team's Santa Cruz summer camp, that he was destined to become one of the real iron men of pro, a sort of counterpart to Lou Gehrig in baseball.

I was the only sportswriter to attend that first practice session more than twenty-five years ago. The other day I called Otto in Auburn—that's gold rush country—where, after buying a ranch near Yuba City, he acquired a thriving fast-food place, and where he now lives with his wife, Sally, and two children.

I asked Jim if he recalled a chat we had that day, and he did. The Raiders were then a hastily formed ragtag group, but Jim said he was proud to be part of a brand-new league. "I'm glad to be a charter member of the AFL, which one day will compete on even terms with the NFL," he predicted. "I really prefer playing with this new outfit."

And he talked as if he meant it. He entered pro football with none of the fanfare and frills of a blue-chip college, high draft choice. NFL scouts considered him too small at 210 pounds to stand the gaff of rugged pro ball, and he wasn't even drafted by that league. How badly they misjudged his durability! As it turned out, he was to prove as tough and rugged as the 49ers' Leo Nomellini.

Otto is a native of Wausau, Wisconsin, a town of about forty thousand, fairly near Green Bay. That's pro football country. A prep star there, he went on to become center linebacker for the University of Miami Hurricanes for three years. He was consistently good, yet not one NFL club would even offer him a free agent contract, let alone draft him.

His only chance was the AFL. Minneapolis drafted him number twenty-five before being admitted into the NFL as the Vikings, when it turned its AFL franchise over to eight greenhorn businessmen in Oakland. Armed with two pairs of football shoes, two flimsy suitcases, a helmet, and an intense desire, Otto reported to Coach Eddie Erdelatz at Santa Cruz.

The odds seemed against Jim's making it, but he did. He stayed for fifteen years, during which time he started every regular season game and wound up making the Pro Football Hall of Fame, the first Raider to do so and only the third AFL athlete to be so honored.

For thirteen straight years Jim was all-Pro, the only all-AFL center in the loop's history. All told, he played 308 games (including those 210 straight regular season battles) and one Super Bowl (the second). Except for 1960 when he wore the number 50 jersey, Jim sported 00, and this unique numeral doubtless helped him gain the attention he deserved. But the recognition he received was primarily because he developed into a superstar.

After a disheartening string of 19 losses in 1961–62, the Raiders bounced back with a 10-4 season in 1963, and during the remainder of Jim's career, amassed the best won-lost mark in pro, winning the AFL championship in 1967 and seven division titles in eight years, through Jim's final season in 1974.

During all these years the Raiders had an outstanding offensive line—Jim was a sure-handed ball snapper, a superior blocker, and he sought out targets beyond the area of a center. But there was more to his success than just technical know-how and sheer determination. Those who played with or against him use such encomiums as "pride," "leadership," "dedication," and "intelligence"—not in the visible rah-rah way, but because he was always in the lineup and showing leadership.

"He loved to win," teammate George Blanda tells us. "He led by example and set the tempo. He gave us an image of discipline, hard work, and hard-nosed football."

Jim was also assigned to call blocking signals for the offense. In one season the Raiders called about 650 plays and Otto was judged to have made only about a dozen errors. "We made few mental errors and Jim Otto was the main reason," Ollie Spencer, Oakland offense coach, proudly explains.

Unlike many stars who try several positions before settling down to one, Jim played center and linebacker at Wausau High and from then on insisted center was his cup of tea. And he wasted little time on his other problem, size. He ballooned from a skinny 210-pounder, adding 30 pounds to his six-foot-two frame.

Jim recalls that the early Raiders days required sacrifices off the field as well as on. Poor locker-room facilities, substandard travel accommodations, and meager fan acceptance, as well as low pay, added to Raiders' discomforts. The team moved from pillar to post like unwanted orphans—first Kezar (where the seagulls often outnumbered the paid customers), then Candlestick, then tiny Youell Field in Oakland, and finally the Oakland Coliseum, which became their home.

If Jim hadn't possessed a strong sense of loyalty he could

have terminated his AFL miseries after just one season, because the same NFL teams who wanted no part of him earlier offered him bigger pay to quit the Raiders. But Jim would have none of it.

Were it not for dozens of injuries, he might have gone on playing a few more years. His medical history could fill an encyclopedia: elbow bone chips, broken nose (ten times), broken jaw, brain concussions, dislocated knee and fingers, severely pinched neck nerve, and three left knee operations (he wound up with essentially an artificial right knee).

Even so, he gave it one more try. Early in the 1974 preseason game against the hated 49ers, the Raiders moved down the field and scored behind Jim's excellent blocking. Then he left the game, never to return.

"I didn't have to quit," he insisted. "I played well, but not well enough. And I wanted to quit when still on top."

Perhaps one thing most remarkable about Otto's pro record was his durability, particularly in view of his manifold injuries. The old Iron Horse played in 308 contests all told. Of his 210 in-season games, he started in every one of them. He's proud of that.

215

What's Become of the Humor?

ONE THING CONSPICUOUS by its absence in today's sports pages is humor. The light and airy anecdotes and banter of yesterday is sadly missing. It's particularly lacking in baseball. Humor doesn't come easily to athletes today, who are too busy counting their money to be bothered by the lighter side.

Most writers, too, are delinquent in the humor department. Perhaps they are too engulfed in the latest developments in drugs, free agent dickerings and bickerings, and players' union strikes and rumors of strikes to be bothered with a search for the laughs fans are so eager to read.

In the bygone days, humor headed the list of "musts" for sportswriters. They strove for witty leads and anecdotes that would make the reader chuckle. Here are a few of these that readily come to mind.

In the old Pacific Coast League days Harry Williams, a baseball writer who later became a long-time president of the loop, wrote this lead for the *Los Angeles Times:* "Arthur Somers Sutherland today pitched his initials off but lost 1 to 0 on a two-hitter."

Then there was the night Smead Jolley, the stumbling, bumbling but affable outfielder and home-run slugger who one season hit over .400 in the Coast League, spoke to an audience of young boys. One asked, seriously, "Mr. Jolley, is it better for a hitter to step forward with his right foot or step to one side?"

216

Jolley mulled over the question for a moment, then replied, "Son, it doesn't pay to be superstitious at the plate."

Then there was the Boosters' Club luncheon of the San Francisco Giants when handsome Bob Shaw, the pitcher, was asked by a buxom young lady from the audience, "You ball players are so young and handsome. Do you like your women a little older than yourself?"

To which Shaw replied, "I do, but my wife doesn't."

This one happened during spring training in Arizona. Babe Pinelli, who had just retired after working behind the plate when Don Larsen pitched his World Series no-hitter, had been a third baseman himself. He liked the fielding of Jim Ray Hart, rookie third sacker, and assumed he was a Caribbean black who spoke little English.

"Me also play third base," Babe began. "Me see you make two great plays today. You field much good and much good with bat." As Babe talked on, Hart just smiled like a Cheshire cat.

Coach Cookie Lavagetto, who was listening to the one-way conversation, was enjoying a good belly laugh. Finally he came over and said, "Hey, Babe, this boy is no Latin black; he's from North Carolina and speaks better English than you."

When the old Coast League Seals arrived in Hana, Maui, to train in 1946, they neglected to bring along an umpire for exhibition games. The only available islander spoke very little English and had even less experience.

In the first game the umpire worked, the pitcher threw one a mile high to Ted Jennings and the islander bawled, "Four ball." A split second later he reversed himself, saying, "Belong out." Jennings naturally squawked, to which the ump explained, "Lookee here, see? Four ball. Yes, sure, but bases all loaded. No room to put fourth man so belong out, you see?"

The Seals radioed the mainland that night for a stateside umpire.

Charlie Dressen swore the following really happened when he managed Oakland's Acorns after leaving the Dodgers. Brick Laws, Oaks owner, sent him to Stockton on the Monday off-day to look over a prospect.

"Okay, son," Dressen told the boy, "let's see how you field." The kid took his place at third base wearing shin guards. "You're a catcher, eh? I thought you played third base," said Dressen.

"I'm a third baseman, you bet," said the rookie, "but I'm a little weak fielding ground balls."

When the Giants were training in Phoenix, Mike McCormick, the promising southpaw, was warming up on the sidelines when a lady came up and said, "You know, Mr. McCormick, I've seen every inning of every game you have pitched for San Francisco. I'd like your autograph."

McCormick signed her program obligingly, and as he was doing so the lady said, "Why, Mr. McCormick, I didn't know you were a left-hander!"

When San Francisco's Joe Orengo, a former cable car conductor, was in the St. Louis Cardinals chain, he received his new contract for the same money he got after a good year the season before. Irately, he sent Branch Rickey, penurious boss of the Cardinals "chain gang," a wire that read, "Before playing for the kind of money you offer I'll quit baseball and take a job picking oranges."

A few hours later Joe got a two-word reply from Rickey that read, "Pick 'em."

One morning at Churchill Downs in Louisville, Alfred Gwynne Vanderbilt stood with a group watching the great Native Dancer work out prepping for the Kentucky Derby. One trainer remarked that he didn't like the way the colt walked off the track after a trial spin.

"I never used to like the way Citation walked off the track either," quipped Vanderbilt, "because he always walked back to the Calumet barn instead of mine."

Joe Engel, one-time president of the Chattanooga club, once pitched for Clark Griffith on the old Washington Senators. He was very wild and Griffith finally called him into the front office and said he was being traded down the river to Minneapolis, then in the minors.

"For whom?" Engel asked.

"For nobody," Griffith answered. "It's an even trade and will strengthen our club."

The New York Yankees, driving into Monterrey, Mexico, arrived at the Central Bus Terminal. The street was lined with Mexicans cheering madly. Stengel was elated, and when the bus pulled up in front of the hotel where the club was stopping overnight, he remarked that the people must be crazy about the Yankees.

"Señor," replied the guide, "it is not the Yanquis that has caused the demonstration. You see, this is the first time the people of Monterrey have ever seen a new Greyhound bus."

Alvin Dark, a very religious man who gives a tithe (10 percent) to the Baptist church, used a biblical quotation as a protest against a called third strike in a game against the old Milwaukee Braves when he was wearing a New York Giants uniform. Umpire Al Barlick told me the story, to wit:

"The count on Dark reached two and two and I called the next pitch a ball. Catcher Del Crandall gave me a growl, but Dark thought the call was great. The next pitch was real close. I called Dark out on a third strike. As he walked away from the plate shaking his head, he muttered, 'The Lord giveth and then the Lord taketh away.' "